Discovering Decimals

Through Cooperative Learning

by Laura Candler

Kagan

Kagan Publishing
P.O. Box 72008
San Clemente, CA 92673-2008
1(800) 933-2667
www.KaganOnline.com

ISBN: 978-1-879097-43-8

Table of Contents

Discovering Decimals

Discovering Decimals

Table of Structures

Discovering Decimals

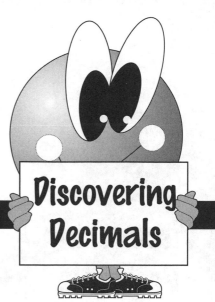

Discovering Decimals

Introduction

Mathematics instruction has undergone a revolution of sorts in the last two decades. The typical math class twenty years ago consisted of neat rows of students laboriously attacking full pages of computation problems, no sound to be heard except the scratching of pencil on paper. Today the typical math class is more likely to consist of small groups of students brandishing calculators as they attack a complex problem, the silence replaced by the noisy hum of discussion.

The mathematics classroom is different because our society is different. Traditional teaching methods produced students who could solve basic computation problems, but who were uncomfortable solving real-life problems. With the advent of calculators and computers, our society leaped into the information age. Our world has become increasingly complex, and the ability to solve complex problems is now more important than simple computational skills.

The National Council of Teachers of Mathematics (NCTM) responded to societal changes by spearheading a curriculum reform movement, resulting in their document *Curriculum and Evaluation Standards for School Mathematics*. New goals outlined in the document include a focus on mathematical reasoning and problem-solving. NCTM also recognizes the need for individuals to communicate mathematically and to develop confidence in one's own mathematical ability. To this end, teachers are encouraged to use cooperative learning strategies and provide multiple opportunities for complex problem solving.

The new standards in math present many challenges for classroom teachers. Many of us were taught in "traditional" math classes where rote memorization was rewarded and working together was discouraged. Yet now we are expected to group our students, teach with manipulatives, and– heaven forbid–encourage calculator use!

How do we as teachers respond to these challenges?

In order to meet the challenges presented by the new curriculum standards, teachers can and should seek out the many resources available to educators. This book is a response to the need for such resources. *Discovering Decimals* offers a variety of easy decimal activities for the cooperative classroom. The activities are simple to implement, and many involve manipulatives and calculators. Some of the activities are designed to enhance computation skills, and others focus primarily on problem-solving. All of the activities, through their cooperative nature, promote communication and confidence in mathematical ability.

Teaching math today is a challenging task, but one that offers many rewards. I always look forward to introducing a new math manipulative . . . my students' enthusiasm is catching! I also enjoy watching my students grow from hesitant problem-solvers to confident problem-attackers. Letting them use a calculator and work in teams empowers them to conquer any problem with confidence. Later, they transfer this feeling of confidence to problems they tackle on their own.

Most of all, I take pride in helping my students grow as a group, teaching them to work cooperatively and appreciate each other's unique strengths. I believe that learning about decimals is important; however, learning to value yourself and others is absolutely essential. Make each day a new adventure for your students . . . both in discovering decimals and learning about themselves!

Reference

National Council of Teachers of Mathematics. *Curriculum and Evaluation Standards for School Mathematics.* The National Council of Teachers of Mathematics, Reston, VA: 1989.

Acknowledgments

I want to thank the many people who helped make this book possible. First, I want to thank Spencer Kagan who developed the structural approach to cooperative learning. His teaching methods provide the foundation for the activities in *Discovering Decimals.* I also want to express appreciation to Miguel Kagan for managing and coordinating the project, especially for the dynamic book design and decimal illustrations. Thanks to Karen Lo Bosco for her contributions to the book design and for her painstaking work of formatting each page. Celso Rodriguez did a wonderful job with the structure illustrations; his artwork brings the structure descriptions to life. I also want to thank Jeanne Stone for her careful work in editing the final manuscript.

Last, but not least, I appreciate several teachers who helped me field-test these activities. Thanks to Jonnie Miller, Sandra Leechford, Rachel Pinkham and Tanya Wornall for their valuable suggestions. They have been wonderfully appreciative and supportive of me throughout the writing of this book. All three are excellent math teachers, and I count myself lucky to work with them!

Chapter 1

Getting Started

How To Use This Book

Introduction

Discovering Decimals *is an activity book, designed to provide a smorgasbord of teaching strategies to help you introduce decimals and build decimal concepts. You'll discover more ideas than you could possibly use in one unit of decimal instruction, so read on to find out how to best make use of this resource.*

 Chapter 1 presents ideas for getting started. The first few pages are a brief overview of cooperative learning basics. If your class is already set up in teams of four, and you are familiar with the structural approach to cooperative learning, skip to the tips on mathematics instruction.

The next few pages provide suggestions for teaching mathematics today. You'll find strategies for introducing decimals, ideas for using manipulatives, tips for motivating problem-solvers, and ways to use learning centers in the math class.

In Chapter 2 you'll find detailed descriptions of each cooperative learning structure. If you are already familiar with these structures, just skim their descriptions and refer to them later as needed.

Chapter 3 contains decimal activities organized sequentially by skill. Each skill offers a variety of activities; scan them and decide upon the approach that best meets your objectives. If your students don't master the skill immediately, return to the section for more reteaching ideas.

Each activity page includes a brief synopsis, a list of materials needed, getting ready ideas, and a step-by-step set of instructions. Many activities have associated blackline master(s) on the following page(s).

In Chapter 4, you'll find frequently used blacklines for patterns as well as directions for creating manipulatives.

 The last section is for your convenience; it contains answers for the worksheets. . . ready-made answer keys at your fingertips!

 Skim the book to locate your favorite activities before you plan your decimal unit. The beauty of the structural approach is that there are many ways to teach the same concept. However, you may feel overwhelmed by all the possibilities if you don't plan ahead!

Using Cooperative Learning Structures

What Is A Structure?

Cooperative learning structures are teaching techniques that can be adapted to almost any subject matter. Many teachers are familiar with simple structures like Think-Pair-Share and RoundRobin. Most are not aware that more than one hundred structures have been identified by Dr. Spencer Kagan, who developed the structural approach used in this book. I have found 14 structures to be particularly useful in teaching decimals. Later, in Chapter 2, each structure listed below is explained in detail, along with hints and tips for success.

How Are Structures Used?

Before reading further, it is important to realize that structures can be divided into "domains of usefulness," or categories according to how

they are used. You'll notice that many structures appear in more than one domain since they are versatile and can be used in more than one way.

Classbuilding Structures...

These structures provide opportunities for students to learn about others in the entire class. They encourage a sense of class spirit by bringing students into contact with each other and helping them value each other's differences as well as similarities.

- ◆ **Line Ups**
- ◆ **Mix-Freeze-Pair**
- ◆ **Mix-N-Match**

Teambuilding Structures...

Teambuilding structures create a sense of team spirit among the members of a group. They are prescribed ways of interaction that lead to a feeling of "we, instead of me." True teambuilders are completely content-free, encouraging students to enjoy each other as individuals without regard to academic abilities.

- ◆ RoundRobin
- ◆ RoundTable

Content Mastery Structures...

Mastery structures are primarily used for review and practice of basic skills. These structures are useful when a problem calls for one specific correct answer. In mathematics, mastery structures are useful for teaching basic computation skills, as well as number theory, geometry, measurement, statistics, and a host of other concepts.

- ◆ Line Ups
- ◆ Mix-Freeze-Pair
- ◆ Mix-N-Match
- ◆ Numbered Heads

Together
- ◆ Pairs Check
- ◆ Pairs Compare
- ◆ Play-N-Switch
- ◆ RallyTable
- ◆ RoundRobin
- ◆ RoundTable
- ◆ Showdown
- ◆ Think-Pair-Share

Thinking and Problem-Solving Structures...

These structures are excellent for encouraging higher-level thinking and developing problem-solving skills. They are designed to promote discussion and expose students to a variety of problem-solving strategies.

- ◆ Numbered Heads
  Together
- ◆ Pairs Compare
- ◆ Send-A-Problem
- ◆ Showdown
- ◆ Teammates Consult
- ◆ Think-Pair-Share

Creating A Cooperative Classroom

Introduction

Creating a cooperative classroom is more involved than simply seating students in groups. Cooperative learning teams are carefully planned and students are given clear guidelines for behavior. Furthermore, a spirit of cooperation is constantly nurtured by teaching students to respect each other and their differences. To do this, provide plenty of opportunities for classbuilding and teambuilding.

Team Formation Ideas...

 Divide your class into teams of four students. Four is the optimal number since a team of four can easily be divided into two pairs.

 Make sure teams are as heterogeneous as possible. Mix boys and girls, students of different ethnic backgrounds, and students varying academic abilities.

Seat team members together by clustering desks, using tables, or seating them on the floor for cooperative activities.

 Form new teams at least every 4 to 6 weeks.

Management Ideas...

Implement a Quiet Signal to use during cooperative activities. Raising your hand, clapping a pattern, and ringing a bell are all effective when used consistently.

Monitor team interactions and encourage equal participation. If teams are having problems getting along, divide them into pairs until they master the social skills needed to work as a team.

Keep team materials in an accessible location. Try placing a basket or margarine tub with glue, markers, crayons, scrap paper, and scissors in the center of each team.

With your students, establish rules for your cooperative classroom and expect students to abide by those rules. Post the rules clearly. (See example.)

Use "classbuilding" structures frequently to foster positive interaction between classmates. Encouraging such interaction helps create a truly cooperative classroom.

Our Cooperative Classroom Rules

1. Listen to each other.
2. Help anyone who asks.
3. Obey the Quiet Signal.
4. Take turns.
5. Share materials.
6. Praise each other. (No put-downs allowed!)

Investigating Decimal Concepts

Introduction

Teaching decimals presents a challenge to most educators, probably due to the abstract nature of the concept. Elementary students have particular difficulty grasping decimal concepts, unless those ideas are presented concretely using hands-on activities. Below you'll find some suggestions for helping students unravel the mystery of decimals.

No matter the age group, start your decimal study by giving students concrete experiences using Base 10 Manipulatives or decimal grids. (More information on manipulatives can be found in the next section.)

 After students use Base 10 Manipulatives, have them draw pictures to represent their Base 10 block arrangements. Drawing what they have done enables them to connect these concrete experiences with the more abstract concepts they will explore later.

 Introduce decimals by reviewing whole number place value and showing how decimal numbers continue the place value pattern. (Moving from left to right, numbers decrease by powers of ten.)

Teach students to read decimals aloud correctly using appropriate place value names. For example, say "Two and seven tenths" instead of "Two point seven." Teaching students to read decimals correctly will help them see decimals as a natural extension of our place value system.

Guide students to find ways that decimals are used in real life (money, measurement, etc.) When introducing decimals, relate tenths and hundredths to dimes and pennies. Asking "What part of a dollar is a penny?" may help some students understand decimal values.

 Help students find connections between decimals and fractions (and percents for older students). Linking decimals, fractions, and percents helps students see the "big picture" in mathematics.

 Use number lines to introduce and reinforce basic decimal concepts.

 Teach concepts using cooperative activities. Structure the activities to provide for individual accountability so that everyone is expected to learn every skill. (The activities in Chapter 3 are highly structured to maximize participation and learning.)

 Involve students in math journal writing on a regular basis. Ask them to explain how they solved a problem and draw pictures to illustrate their solution. Or ask them to describe how someone might use a particular decimal skill in everyday life. Reflecting in journals helps students learn to "speak" the language of mathematics.

 Assess student learning frequently using independent "quick quizzes" to make sure everyone is mastering the necessary skills. These mini quizzes do not have to be graded— they may consist of only 3 or 4 items and can be used for informal assessment.

Teaching Decimals With Manipulatives

Introduction

Math manipulatives may be store-bought for general use or homemade for a particular activity. In any event, manipulatives are essential to math instruction. Fortunately, most decimal concepts can be taught with relatively few manipulatives, and most of those items can be made if funds aren't available to purchase them.

Manipulatives Needed For Teaching Decimals...

- ◆ Calculators (minimum 1 per team, optimal 1 per person)
- ◆ Base 10 Manipulatives (an inexpensive card stock classroom set can be purchased from *Kagan Publishing*)
- ◆ Base 10 Place Value Mats (directions on page 154)
- ◆ Play money (coin pattern on page 163)

Creating Manipulatives...

Many of the items above can be created using the directions and patterns at the back of this book. In addition, hands-on materials needed for particular activities are located next to the activity in Chapter 3. You may want to cut out and laminate these materials for future use before the lesson. Or if you are short on time, let your students cut out their own manipulatives just prior to the activity.

Many of the activities in this book use Base 10 manipulatives. If you did not purchase Base 10 Manipulatives from *Kagan Publishing* with this book, you may purchase them separately. If you prefer to make your own classroom set, use the patterns on pages 155 & 156. Copy enough manipulatives so every team has their own set. These patterns can also be used to make overhead transparencies. Colored transparency film works especially well. You'll also need to prepare a number of Place Value Mats; depending on the activity you may need one per person or one per team.

Storing Manipulatives...

Manipulatives may be conveniently stored in everything from ice cream buckets to plastic baby wipe containers. Homemade manipulatives created for a particular activity are easily stored by dividing materials into team sets and placing them into plastic bags. The entire set of 7 or 8 bags can then be stored in a labeled manila envelope and filed for future use. Calculators can be stored in shoe bags, pocket charts, or as team sets in plastic bags.

Distributing and Collecting Manipulatives...

Valuable lesson time can be lost if manipulatives are not distributed in an organized manner. If time allows, materials can be counted out and placed on team trays before the lesson. Another option is assigning a Materials Monitor from each team who is responsible for getting the materials and returning them to their proper places after the lesson. Rotate the role of Materials Monitor on a daily or weekly basis.

Motivating Reluctant Problem-Solvers

Introduction

Students often arrive in our classrooms with a fear of mathematical problem solving. They associate word problems with frustration, never having experienced the pleasure of working through and finally solving a difficult problem. Previous teachers may have insisted that they work every problem out by hand, so that even if they understood how to solve a problem, careless errors prevented them from finding a correct solution.

To become confident problem-solvers, students must conquer their fears and approach problem solving with a new attitude. These strategies will motivate even the most reluctant problem solvers.

 Make calculators available to students during *every single problem-solving session*. When relieved of the drudgery of paper and pencil computation, students begin to view each new problem as a fun challenge.

Show students that you value their efforts, not just their correct answers. The easiest way to do this is to have students explain their answers in writing. Give at least half credit for a correct method, even when the answer is wrong.

 Allow students to solve problems in cooperative groups, especially at first. Use structures like Numbered Heads Together, Showdown, Teammates Consult, and Pairs Compare. Students who have no idea how to tackle a problem quickly learn from students who verbalize their methods. (Don't forget to provide independent practice also!)

Be spontaneous enough to stop and investigate real-life problems when they arise. Planning a field trip, graphing attendance during a chicken pox epidemic, and figuring how many days will be needed to finish a book are examples of problems your students may enjoy investigating.

Post a list of Problem-Solving Strategies (page 13) and remind students to refer to it when they get stuck. Just knowing that there are alternate ways to solve a problem may help some students.

Look for more than one correct solution to a problem. Praise students who can justify alternate answers.

Teach students to find at least two ways to solve a problem. Reward students for discovering more than one method of arriving at a correct answer.

 Ask students to illustrate a problem when they are having trouble finding an answer. Sometimes just drawing the parts of the problem will help them discover the solution.

Treat problem-solving as an adventure filled with risks as well as rewards.

Problem-Solving Strategies

- ◆ Guess and check
- ◆ Write a number sentence
- ◆ Make an organized list
- ◆ Make a table
- ◆ Look for a pattern
- ◆ Solve a simpler problem
- ◆ Work backward
- ◆ Draw a picture
- ◆ Act it out
- ◆ Use manipulatives

Enriching Decimal Instruction With Centers

Introduction

The decimal lessons in this book are designed to be taught to whole classes seated in cooperative learning teams, but many of the activities can be adapted to learning centers. Centers are an important part of many primary classrooms; however, upper elementary and middle school students can also benefit from this form of instruction. Math centers empower students by giving them choices and helping to meet individual needs.

What is a Learning Center?

A learning center does not need a colorful display or a costly set of manipulatives. A center may be as simple as a deck of cards and a sheet of directions. Depending on the type of center, the whole class may participate simultaneously, or students may choose a particular center after finishing regular classwork. These two types of centers are described below.

Rotation Learning Centers...

Rotation Learning Centers are excellent for an end-of-unit review. To prepare for the lesson, gather directions and materials for six or seven different decimal review activities. For example,

one center may consist of a deck of cards and directions for Decimal War. Another center may have materials for a Showdown activity on rounding decimals. An easy way to collect materials for this culminating activity is to save manipulatives from the cooperative lessons you teach throughout the unit.

With Rotation Learning Centers, the entire class participates simultaneously. Assign each team to a different station, and allow 10–15 minutes to complete the activities at that center. Then call time and have teams rotate to the next station. Students love the chance to do all their favorite cooperative decimal activities again, and it's great test preparation.

Learning Choice Centers...

Sometimes called "Choosing Centers," these centers are usually set up at a separate table and students choose to visit them when they finish other assignments. Learning Choice Centers may be used for enrichment and remediation; in fact, a single activity may serve as a review for one student and a challenge for others. Many of the cooperative decimal activities in this book may be adapted for use in Learning Choice Centers.

Structures that work well for this are Play-N-Switch, RallyTable, RoundTable, and Showdown. You might choose to introduce a decimal skill to the whole class using one structure, then prepare a related center activity using a different structure. Store laminated directions and materials for each activity in a manila envelop, and keep them on file for future use.

Chapter 2

Cooperative Learning Structures

Structure
1

Line-Ups

Overview...

Line-Ups is a simple structure that's easy to implement. Students love it because participating in a Line-Up allows them to get out of their seat and mix with other students. Teachers enjoy using Line-Ups because the structure is effective in teaching students to sequence information and contributes to a positive classroom atmosphere.

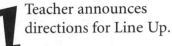 **Steps...**

1 Teacher announces directions for Line Up.

2 Students line up according to directions.

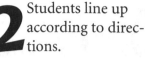 **Hints...**

- **Number Signs** - Write numbers on individual chalkboards, large index cards, or slips of paper. Have students hold the number signs as they line up in numerical order.

- **Countdown** - After lining up, have students orally announce their number as the class counts down from the largest to smallest number. All class members should listen to hear if the numbers are in the correct order.

 **Variations...**

- **Value Line-Ups** - Students line up according to their relative feelings about a particular issue. The teacher calls out a question such as "How do you feel about studying decimals?" Then the teacher identifies the ends of the Line Up, such as agree/disagree or like it/hate it. Students line up accordingly.

Mix-Freeze-Pair

Structure
2

Overview...

Mix-Freeze-Pair is one of my favorite structures because it serves two purposes. It's excellent for improving class spirit as well as strengthening academic skills. Since students are constantly mixing and forming new pairs, they become exposed to different perspectives and problem-solving methods. It's also a great structure to use when students are restless after sitting still for long periods of time.

Steps...

1 The teacher says "Mix!" and students mill around the room.

2 The teacher announces "Freeze" and students stop.

3 The teacher says "Pair" and students find a partner.

4 Pairs are given time to discuss a teacher-provided topic or solve a problem.

5 Students mix, freeze, and pair again as prompted by the teacher.

Hints...

- **Odd Number of Students** - If you have an odd number of students, allow one group of three during each round.

- **Link Arms** - When you say "Pair," have students link arms loosely with their partner. That will keep students from attempting to pair with a person who is already someone else's partner.

- **Classbuilding** - Encourage students to pair with a different person for each round of the activity. Explain that one goal of the activity is for students to get to know their classmates better.

Mix-N-Match

Structure
3

Overview...

Mix-N-Match promotes positive interaction between classmates in addition to content mastery. Students mix around the room, exchanging cards that have matching problems and answers. After the teacher says "Freeze!" students stop and find their match. Cards with matching problems and answers can be created by the students or prepared in advance by the teacher. Since students trade cards throughout the activity, Mix-N-Match can be repeated over and over with students constantly being exposed to new problems.

Steps...

1 Students mix around the room and trade cards with different students they encounter.

2 Teacher announces "Freeze!" and students stop.

3 Teacher calls "Match!" and students find their match.

4 Play again.

Mix-N-Match Patterns

| Problem | Answer |
| Problem | Answer |

Hints...

- **Matching Pairs Move to Edges** - When students find their match, have them move to the edges of the room. This leaves the center free for students who still haven't found a partner.

- **Mix-N- Match Patterns** - Save time and eliminate confusion by using the blank **Mix-N-Match Patterns** (page 166). Write problems on the squares and answers on the octagons. Students will be able to find their match more quickly since they will be looking for a particular shape.

- **Color Coding** - Write problems on one color paper and answers on another. This eliminates confusion and allows students to find their match more quickly.

- **Reusable Cards** - Use card stock, construction paper, or index cards to prepare the Mix-N-Match cards. Laminate them and store them for future use.

- **Odd Numbers** - If you have an odd number of students, you can solve the problem of uneven matches in several ways. You may want to even-up the numbers by participating in the activity yourself. Or you can pair two students as "twins" who always travel together.

Structure
4

Numbered Heads Together

Overview...

Numbered Heads Together is a classic cooperative learning structure. Students in teams literally put their heads together to solve a problem or answer a ques-tion. The teacher calls a number and students with that number stand to re-spond. When working with math problems, it's helpful to use a variation in which students write their own an-swer first before discussing their ideas with the team.

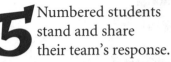

Steps...

1 Students, in teams, number off 1 to 4.

2 The teacher asks a question or states a problem.

3 Students put their heads together to discuss responses.

4 The teacher calls a random number.

5 Numbered students stand and share their team's response.

Hints...

- **Stand Alone** - Make sure students "stand alone," during the last step and are not allowed to receive help from team members after a number is called. Enforcing this rule will encourage students to pay attention during the team discussion so they will know the answer if called upon.

- **Team Response Boards** - Use small team chalkboards during the last step

of Numbered Heads. Have the designated student write his or her answer on the board to hold up when called upon. If you don't have small chalkboards, you can laminate 10" x 12" pieces of poster board and let students write on them with overhead pens. You can also cut a sheet of smooth white paneling into sections and let students use dry-erase markers on them.

bers - Use a Numbered Heads spinner or a Student Selector to choose a number (both are available from Kagan Publishing). If you don't have a spinner, roll a regular 6-sided die. If a 5 or 6 comes up, call it "teacher choice" and select a number that hasn't responded so far.

Variations...

- **Numbered Heads With Writing** - To increase active participation, ask students to write their own answers before sharing them with the team. In problem solving, give a few minutes for individual problem solving before you allow team discussion.

- **Traveling Heads** - After calling a number, have the numbered students stand and move to a new team. Ask them to share their answer with their new team, who gives help or praise as needed. Call on a representative from one or two teams to give the an-

swer to the class. For each round, call a new number and announce a different number of teams for the traveler to move. For example, "Person #2 travel 3 teams over." This way the teams will be randomly mixed after several rounds.

Pairs Check

Structure 5

keep the rest of the team on track. All students benefit from helping and coaching each other. Students who are having difficulty often learn more easily from other students who have mastered a skill. Students who have mastered a skill are more likely to retain their knowledge after teaching it to someone else.

For easy management, divide each team of four into two sets of partners. Name one person in each pair Partner A and the other Partner B. Give each pair one **Pairs Check Form** worksheet (page 165). Each pair works the problems simultaneously, only stopping to compare answers after completing each row. A checkmark is placed in the box after teammates celebrate correct answers for that row.

Overview...

Pairs Check involves students alternately working in pairs and teams. Students first solve one or two problems as a pair, then check their answers with their teammates. The pair work results in a high level of on-task behavior. In addition, the frequent "team checks" ensure a high degree of mathematical accuracy. No matter how difficult the task, at least one student on the team is likely to have mastered the skill and will

Steps...

1 Partner A works the first problem as Partner B coaches and praises.

2 Partner B works the next problem as Partner A coaches and praises.

3 Pairs compare and discuss answers.

4 Teams celebrate correct answers or resolve differences, placing a check mark in the box next to the completed problems.

5 Pairs repeat steps as they complete the worksheet.

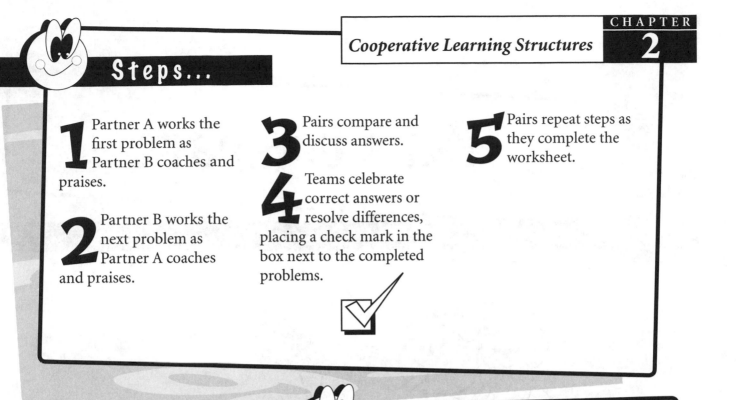

Hints...

• **Pairs Check Form** - Make copies of the blank **Pairs Check Form** (page 165) to use with your own problems. Using a **Pairs Check Form** worksheet helps students stay focused and together as a team.

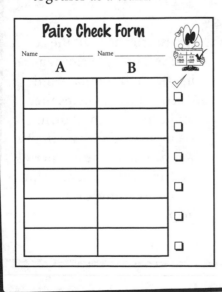

Pairs Check Form

Name _____ Name _____

A	B	
		☐
		☐
		☐
		☐
		☐
		☐

• **Verbalizing Steps** - Encourage students to talk out loud as they solve their problems. For example, "Three plus nine is twelve. I put down the two and carry the one." As they talk, their partner should be listening to the steps to provide help if needed.

• **Patient Waiting** - The most difficult task part for many students involves waiting for the other pair of students to complete

a row of problems. Teach students to wait patiently in a non-disruptive manner. You may need to change the pairs or offer help if one set always finishes first.

• **Half Sheets** - If students don't finish in class and you want to assign the other problems for homework, have students cut the worksheet vertically down the center of the page.

Structure
6

Pairs Compare

Overview...

Pairs Compare is a simple structure, often used in combination with RallyTable. Students in teams are divided into pairs. They work with their partner to complete an activity, then both sets of pairs compare and discuss their answers. If pairs are allowed to compare across teams, this structure can serve as a "sponge" after almost any partner activity. Pairs which complete assignments quickly can use the extra time to compare answers with any others in the class who are also finished. Since those who finish first don't necessarily have all the correct responses, encouraging them to compare and discuss answers helps them find errors on their own. Using Pairs Compare in this way also frees the teacher to work with students who need more time or extra help.

Steps...

1 Pairs complete an activity with their partner.

2 Pairs compare responses with another pair.

3 All four students discuss and resolve differences in answers.

Hints...

- **Heterogeneous Pairs** - Pair strong students with weaker students for the first step. By making heterogeneous pairs, students are more likely to finish at about the same time as their teammates.

- **Sponge Activity** - If you use Pairs Compare as a sponge activity, remember that slower-working pairs may not have time to compare and discuss answers with another pair. Be sure to monitor their progress carefully.

- **Content Mastery** - When using this structure for content mastery, follow Pairs Compare with a quick class check. Pairs may have the same answers, but those answers aren't necessarily correct!

- **Making Corrections** - Allow pairs to make corrections to their papers during the comparing stage if they discover a mistake. However, be sure to hold students accountable for such changes by asking them to explain what they did wrong and by giving them an individual quiz later.

- **List Writing** - Pairs Compare is the structure of choice when having students write lists. Ask a question such as, "How many ways do people use decimals in everyday life?" or "How many ways can you find to solve this problem?" Give each pair one sheet of paper and have the partners take turns adding items to their list of responses. Next, ask pairs to compare with the pair across the table. Finally, as a team challenge, all four continue to add items to the list.

Structure 7

Play-N-Switch

to improve skills. Encourage students to be honest and play fair at all times.

Play-N-Switch games are often taught to the entire class and played simultaneously. After each pair finishes a game, they praise each other and discuss winning strategies. New pairs form and individuals test out their ideas on different opponents.

In addition to whole class use, Play-N-Switch is ideal for learning centers. After introducing the activity to the entire class, leave materials in an easily accessible place. When students have finished other assignments, they can challenge each other to whatever skill game is available.

Overview...

Play-N-Switch can be described in just two words: cooperative competition. Students play a math game with a partner, cooperating and assisting each other in order to sharpen skills and develop winning strate-gies. Teachers can foster the friendly spirit of competition by resisting the urge to award points or tangible prizes to the winners. Instead, remind students that everyone is a winner since Play-N-Switch is a fun way

Steps...

1 Pairs play a skill game together.

2 Players praise and congratulate each other.

3 Players discuss winning strategies.

4 New pairs form for next game.

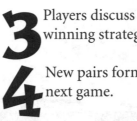

Hints...

• **Equal Ability Pairing** - It's usually best to pair students with similar abilities for Play-N-Switch. A weak student who is consistently paired with strong students may lose confidence in his or her math abilities.

• **Reward Cooperation** - Instead of rewarding winners, call attention to students who are cooperating and playing fair.

• **Teacher Plays** - Occasionally join in and play a game yourself, especially if you have an odd number of students. Students become excited about math games when they see their teacher enthusiastically involved.

• **Don't Overdo It** - Math games have their place as an instructional tool, but too much emphasis on competitive games could break down team spirit or class spirit.

• **Random Pairing** - During the "Switch" use random methods of pairing students. For example, do a Mix-Freeze-Pair, with students finding a new Play-N-Switch partner each round. Or use Mix-N-Match with matching numbered cards. Partners with matching cards find each other and become partners for a round of Play-N-Switch.

Variations...

• **Partner Play-N-Switch** - Sometimes pairs of students enjoying playing together against other pairs. Partner Play-N-Switch is great when the math skills involved are difficult. Students in pairs should take turns through out the game.

Structure
8

RallyTable

Overview...

RallyTable is a simple, but extremely useful, structure for teaching mathematics. Students work in pairs, taking turns to work problems or complete a task. RallyTable is a variation of RoundTable, a structure that involves the full team of four or five students. However, I consider RallyTable to be even more powerful than the original structure. Students working in pairs tend to be directly involved with the task for a greater percentage of the time. RallyTable is also perfect for students who need practice with social skills; group dynamics are simpler in pairs than teams of four.

Steps...

1 The teacher assigns a task or set of math problems.

2 Students in pairs take turns completing the task or working the problems.

Hints...

- **Heterogeneous Pairing** - Plan your pairs in advance rather than assigning them randomly. Make sure that students with weak math skills are paired with stronger math students.

- **Pairs Compare** - Many RallyTable activities can be followed by a "Pairs Compare." This serves as a "sponge" activity to absorb extra time for faster pairs. It also enhances the learning process as pairs discuss their answers with others who have also finished.

- **Color Coding** - Ask students to use different colored pencils for writing their responses. If they sign their name in the same color, you'll know who wrote what.

- **RallyTable Worksheet Practice** - Most prepared math worksheets can be adapted for RallyTable practice. Just duplicate one worksheet for each pair and have them pass it back and forth as they work.

- **Assessment** - RallyTable activities should be used for informal assessment only. Grading these activities would be inappropriate and unfair to both students.

Structure
9

RoundRobin

Overview...

RoundRobin is a simple structure that may be inserted anywhere into a lesson. In this structure, the teacher poses a question or topic and students take turns responding. This format is not designed for true discussion; it's simply an organized and fair way of letting everyone tell their point of view or answer. RoundRobin can be used to introduce an activity with a thought-provoking question or it can provide a moment of review at the end of a lesson. Round-Robin can also be used for oral practice of basic skills such as reading decimals or estimating answers. In addition, this structure is excellent for having students report answers to homework problems.

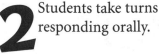

Steps...

1 Teacher asks question or poses problem.

2 Students take turns responding orally.

Hints...

- **Number Off** - Number students off from 1 to 4 within their teams. When you ask them to RoundRobin a response, tell the number of the person who will respond first. Don't always start with Person #1!

- **Active Listening** - This structure is perfect for teaching active listening skills. Remind students to look at the team member who is speaking and to give them their full attention.

- **Time Limits** - When students are giving open-ended answers to a question, assign a time limit for each person to speak. Usually 1 or 2 minutes per person is sufficient, and this simple adaptation will keep one person from monopolizing the team time.

Variations...

- **RoundRobin with Manipulatives** - Sometimes it's helpful to use manipulatives to prompt responses in RoundRobin. For example, a stack of problem cards can be placed face down in the center of the team. Students take turns flipping over the top card and responding to the problem.

- **RallyRobin** - RallyRobin follows the same steps as RoundRobin; however, RallyRobin is used with pairs of students rather than teams of four.

Structure
10

RoundTable

Overview...

RoundTable, like RallyTable, is simple, yet versatile. The only difference between the two structures is that RoundTable is used with full teams of four and RallyTable is used with pairs. Both structures can be summed up in two words: "taking turns." RoundTable has many applications in math. For example, students can take turns writing answers to math problems, sorting manipulatives, or performing a hands-on task.

RoundTable is sometimes confused with RoundRobin; however, RoundRobin responses are oral, whereas RoundTable responses always involve writing or performing a task.

1 The teacher assigns a task or set of math problems.

2 Students in teams take turns completing the assignment.

Hints...

- **Active Involvement** - The most difficult part of this structure for some students is waiting for their turn. Remind them to stay actively involved by watching their teammates respond while they wait for their turn. If the wait time seems to be a problem, restructure the activity by dividing each team into two sets of partners and using RallyTable.

- **RoundTable Worksheet Practice** - Many math worksheets can be used for RoundTable practice activities. Just duplicate one copy per team instead of one per person and have students pass the worksheet around the table to complete.

- **Assessment** - RoundTable activities should never be graded. They are for practice only.

Structure 11

Send-A-Problem

Overview...

Send-A-Problem is an excellent tool for motivating students to enjoy problem solving. Each team is given a set of one or more problems to solve. After each team records their solutions, the problems are rotated to new teams. The game-like atmosphere of this structure guarantees that students will enjoy any mathematics lesson taught with Send-A-Problem.

Steps...

1 Each team is given a different problem (or set of problems.) Students in teams number off from 1 to 4. Person #1 becomes the first Leader.

2 The Leader reads the first problem aloud.

3 Everyone discusses the problem and attempts to solve it.

4 The Leader checks individual answers and guides team to agree on one solution. The Leader records the team answer.

5 If the team was given a set of problems, the Leader follows steps 2 - 4 with each problem.

6 When all teams are ready, the Leader delivers the set of problems to the new Leader (Person #2) on the next team. Continue as time allows, rotating Leaders for each round.

Hints...

- **Student-Generated Problems** - Students enjoy making up their own problems to send to other teams. Give each student an index card and assign a topic to the class (such as Sports Problems). Ask each student to create one problem, then write the problem on one side of the index card and the answer on the other. Have them swap problems with a teammate to check for clarity and accuracy. Follow the same basic Send-A-Problem steps, with one variation. Instead of writing each answer on a worksheet, the Leader checks the solution by turning over the index card. If the answers don't agree, the team continues to work on the problem.

- **Send-A-Problem Activities from Worksheets** - You can use worksheets from teacher activity books and reproducible magazines to create your own Send-A-Problem lessons. Simply cut the worksheet into strips, with one problem to a strip. Number the strips and have the first Leader on each team number an answer page in the same manner.

- **Calculator Use** - Don't forget to let students use calculators when solving complex word problems. This allows them to focus on thinking skills without become anxious about their computation skills.

- **Role Cards** - Make a role card for the Leader on each team. Fold an index card to make a tent and write the word "Leader" on both sides. This role card is passed around the team to identify the Leader for each round.

- **Assessment** - Send-A-Problem answer sheets should not be graded. This structure is excellent for practice, but individual accountability is fairly low so it wouldn't be fair to grade team answers. However, you will probably want to collect the answer sheets and check them as an informal assessment.

Structure
12

Showdown

Overview...

Showdown is an excellent structure for developing both computation and problem solving skills. Its best feature is a strong emphasis on individual accountability. The teacher assigns a set of problems, and everyone works the first problem independently. Then team members take part in a Showdown by holding up their answers for their team to check. Everyone compares answers and discusses problem-solving strategies. Because students individually struggle with each problem, they are more focused when they finally discuss their answers. Another advantage of this structure is its student-directed format, which frees the teacher to monitor and assist where needed.

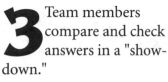

Steps...

1 Teacher assigns a set of math problems.

2 Each student works the first problem individually.

3 Team members compare and check answers in a "showdown."

4 Teammates discuss strategies and celebrate correct answers.

5 Students repeat steps with remaining problems.

Hints...

- **Individual Response Boards** - Having students work problems on individual chalkboards or slates is helpful. Students can more easily see each other's work during the "showdown" stage of the activity. Using chalkboards also conserves paper.

- **Task Cards** - To help students focus on one math problem at a time, the problems can be written on index cards or slips of paper and stacked face down in the center of the team. Use the blank **Showdown Task Card** (page 164) form and write one problem in each block. Duplicate one sheet per team and have students cut them apart on the dotted lines to form cards.

- **Turn Captain** - Assign the rotating role of Turn Captain. This person turns over the top card and leads one round of Showdown.

- **Recording Answers** - Have the Turn Captain record the team answer on the problem card or a numbered sheet of paper. At the end of the activity, collect the cards or paper to check for mathematical accuracy.

Teammates Consult

Structure
13

does the written explanation serve as a deterrent to "hitchhiking," the written responses provide insight into a student's understanding of the problem.

This structure is adaptable to any subject, but when I use it in math I refer to it as "Mathematicians Consult." The steps are somewhat involved at first, so I usually place an overhead transparency of the steps on the projector for students to refer to as they work (page 44). I have also found that this structure requires careful monitoring to keep it from dissolving into a groupwork activity in which one person does all the thinking. Despite these problems, the structure is so powerful when used properly that I find its benefits far outweigh its drawbacks.

Overview...

Teammates Consult is one of my favorite structures for problem solving. All students are given a copy of the same problem-solving assignment. As they work through the problems one-by-one, students are encouraged to discuss methods and share strategies. However, all students are held individually accountable for their answers. The power of this structure lies in the fact that after the team discussion *each student must individually explain the steps of the solution in writing*. Not only

Steps...

1 Everyone places their pencils and calculators in the center of the team.

2 Person #1 becomes the first Leader and reads the first problem aloud.

3 Everyone discusses strategies for solving the problem.

4 The Leader asks, "Does everyone understand how to solve the problem?"

5 If anyone answers "No," students continue the discussion.

6 When everyone is ready, students use calculators to solve the problem. Then they write their own answer **without talking**. Everyone does not have to write the same answer.

7 Students put their and calculators pencils back in the center of team.

8 Next person becomes the new Leader and reads the second problem. The activity continues until all problems are solved.

Hints...

- **Pencil Cups** - Place a large plastic cup in the center of each team. Students can put their pencils in the cup during the discussion. Seeing four pencils in the cup is a visual reminder that talking is allowed. When the cup is empty, there should be **no talking!**

- **Monitor Carefully** - Teammate's Consult has many steps, and students tend to break the rules frequently until they learn this structure. They need lots of reminders that they are not allowed to talk when they are writing. (This ensures that students participate in the discussion since they know they will not have help later.) If one team continues to break the rules, have them separate their desks and finish the assignment independently.

- **Challenging Problems Only** - Teammates Consult is best used with challenging problems and activities that require written responses. This structure would not be appropriate for simple computation worksheets, because it would be difficult to prevent students from just copying each other's answers without doing the work.

- **Grading** - Since each student is held individually accountable by having to write explanations, you can feel comfortable collecting the finished worksheets and grading them. Let students know in advance if you plan to grade the assignment, and remind them that the entire team does not have to agree on the answer.

- **Mathematicians Consult Form** - Create your own problem-solving worksheets by writing word problems in the boxes on the blank **Mathematicians Consult Form** (page 45)

Mathematicians Consult

1. Everyone places pencils and calculators in the center of the team.

2. Leader reads the first problem.

3. Everyone discusses strategies for solving the problem.

4. Leader asks, "Does everyone understand how to solve the problem?"

5. If anyone answers "No," continue the discussion.

6. When everyone is ready, they use their calculators to solve the problem. Then they write their own answer and explanation. **NO TALKING!** (Everyone does not have to write the same answer.)

7. Next person becomes new Leader.

Mathematicians Consult
Problem Solving

Name_____

Problem 1	Answer: _____
	Explanation: _____
	_____
	_____
	_____
	_____
	_____

Problem 2	Answer: _____
	Explanation: _____
	_____
	_____
	_____
	_____
	_____

Problem 3	Answer: _____
	Explanation: _____
	_____
	_____
	_____
	_____
	_____

Problem 4	Answer: _____
	Explanation: _____
	_____
	_____
	_____
	_____
	_____

Structure 14

Think-Pair-Share

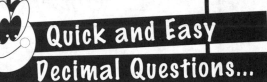

Quick and Easy Decimal Questions...

- What do you already know about decimals?
- What strategy would you use to solve this problem?
- How do people use decimals in every day life?
- In the number 34.786, what digit is in the tenths place?
- In what way are decimals like fractions? How are they different?
- What have you learned today about decimals?
- If the sales tax is 6%, how could you use decimals to figure the tax on $1.45?
- What pattern do you notice when we multiply a decimal by 10, 100, or 1000?
- How would your life be different if we didn't have decimals?
- What did you find most difficult in our decimal study this week?

Overview...

Think-Pair-Share is a favorite of many teachers because it's easy to implement and can be used over and over without advanced preparation. This structure is excellent when you want pairs of students to interact with each other and then with the class as a whole. It's ideal for stimulating discussion on any topic or question. When solving math problems, use the Think-Write-Pair-Share variation. Adding in the writing step encourages students to think on their own before working with a partner.

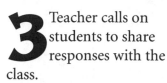

Steps...

1 Teacher poses question or discussion topic.

2 Students pair with a partner to discuss responses.

3 Teacher calls on students to share responses with the class.

Hints...

- **Monitor Carefully -** When you first start using Think-Pair-Share, some students may feel uncomfortable talking with someone they don't know well. Mill around the room and encourage shy students to talk.

- **Assign Partners -** Assign partners in advance to encourage students to

talk with different people. Also, just asking them to "turn to a partner" may leave some students out.

- **Change Partners -** Don't always assign students to the same partner. You can have them pair sideways one time and across the table the next. You can even have students rotate to new seats. If you want

random partners, use Mix-Freeze-Pair.

- **Accountability -** For individual accountability, call on students randomly during the class sharing stage. If you want them to really listen to each other, ask students to tell *what their partner said* during the discussion.

Variations...

- **Timed Pair Share -** During the pair discussion part of Think-Pair-Share, assign one person to talk first for a set time while the other person listens. Call time, and have them switch roles. This ensures the equal participation of both students.

- **Think-Write-Pair-Share** - After posing the problem or question, give students time to think and write their own answer before turning to their partner. The quality of the discussion that follows will be greatly improved.

- **Think-Pair-Square -** This variation provides a way to "tighten up" an unstructured team discussion. First, each person thinks of his or her own answer, then students pair to discuss their ideas. Finally, all four students share their ideas and discuss the topic further.

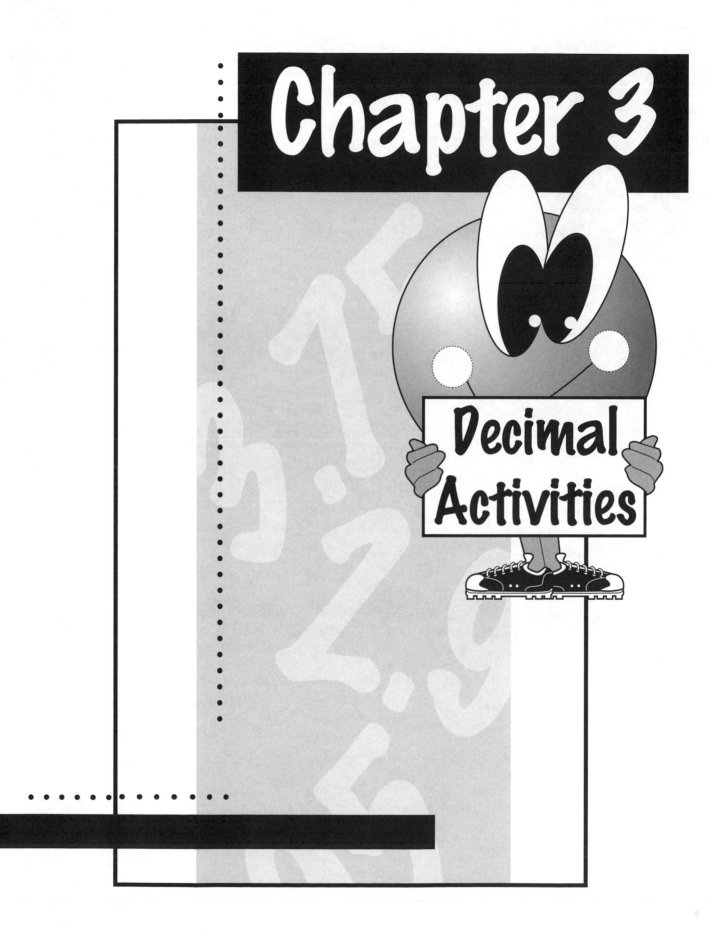

Chapter 3

Decimal Activities

Build It

Team members take turns putting Base 10 manipulatives on a Place Value Mat in order to build a decimal number.

Cubes	Flats	Rods	Units

S t e p s . . .

1 Number students off within teams from 1 to 4. Give each team a set of materials and assign each person one type of manipulative by number. (Start by assigning the units to #1, the rods to #2, the flats to #3, and the cubes to #4.) Put the **Place Value Mat** in the center of the team.

2 Write a decimal number on the overhead transparency or board. (See **Build It Numbers** at right.)

3 Show students one flat and tell them that it represents one whole. Hold up a rod and derive its value by asking "What part of the whole is this?" (one tenth) Explain the meanings of the unit (hundredths) and cube (tens) by using similar questioning strategies. Use one team's **Place Value Mat** to demonstrate how to place the manipulatives in the top row to represent the number you wrote. The bottom row will not be needed.

Build It Numbers
23.45
7.04
9.23
14.8
20.09
3.63
0.94
24.62

4 Write a new number on the board. Students take turns placing manipulatives in their proper locations on the **Place Value Mat**, starting with the hundredths place (units).

5 Check each team's **Place Value Mat** as they finish.

6 Repeat the activity and rotate roles. Students slide their manipulatives to the person on their left so that everyone has a new item. Write another number on the board, have students take turns placing manipulatives, and check the

Cooperative Structure

RoundTable

Materials

- **Base 10 Manipulatives** (1 set per team)
- **Base 10 Place Value Mat** (1 per team)

Getting Ready

Make sure you have enough **Base 10 Manipulatives** (pages 155-156) for each team to have at least 2 cubes, 9 flats, 9 rods, and 9 units. Prepare a **Place Value Mat** (page 154) for each team. Introduce students to decimals by reviewing place value concepts for whole numbers and teaching them that tenths and hundredths follow the same pattern. Develop this concept as you teach the lesson.

Build It

Cubes	Flats	Rods	Units

mats as before. Continue until everyone is comfortable with decimal place value concepts.

Hints & Variations...

• **Individuals Illustrate Responses** - After each round, ask students to draw their Base 10 arrangement in a math journal or on a sheet of paper. Later in the activity, have students illustrate the decimal number on paper before the team builds it. This simple step ensures that students are held individually accountable for learning the concepts rather than just putting manipulatives on a mat.

• **Handling Manipulatives** - Placing the rods and units in small plastic bags helps students pass the manipulatives around the team without losing items.

• **Cooperative Play** - If you are using three-dimensional Base 10 blocks, you'll find students more attentive to the lesson if you give them 5 minutes of Cooperative Play with the materials before you begin. Kids just can't seem to resist building things with Base 10 blocks! After their play time is over, enforce a "hands-off" rule during the activity unless they are actually placing a piece on the mat.

Place Value Strip

3 7 4 . 0 6 5

Place Value Partners

Students work in pairs to build a number by putting digits in their correct places.

Cooperative Structure

RallyTable

Materials

• 1 **Place Value Strip** per pair
• 1 Set of **Place Value Number Cards** per pair
• **Place Value Strip** and **Place Value Number Cards** for the teacher

Getting Ready

Duplicate one **Place Value Strip** (page 55) and one set of **Place Value Number Cards** (page 54) for each pair. Prepare transparencies of those materials for yourself, or laminate a copy of the **Place Value Strip** to use with an overhead pen instead.

S t e p s . . .

1 Divide your class into pairs and seat partners side by side.

2 Give each pair a blank **Place Value Strip** and a set of **Place Value Number Cards**.

3 Digit-by-digit, build a target number by calling out a digit and its place. For example, "Put your 8 in the tenths place." (Simultaneously build the target number on the overhead projector with the lamp turned off.)

4 Students in pairs take turns placing the correct digit in its assigned place.

5 After all the numbers are placed, reveal the target number and have students read it aloud. Continue building target numbers until students are comfortable with decimal place value.

Place Value Number Cards

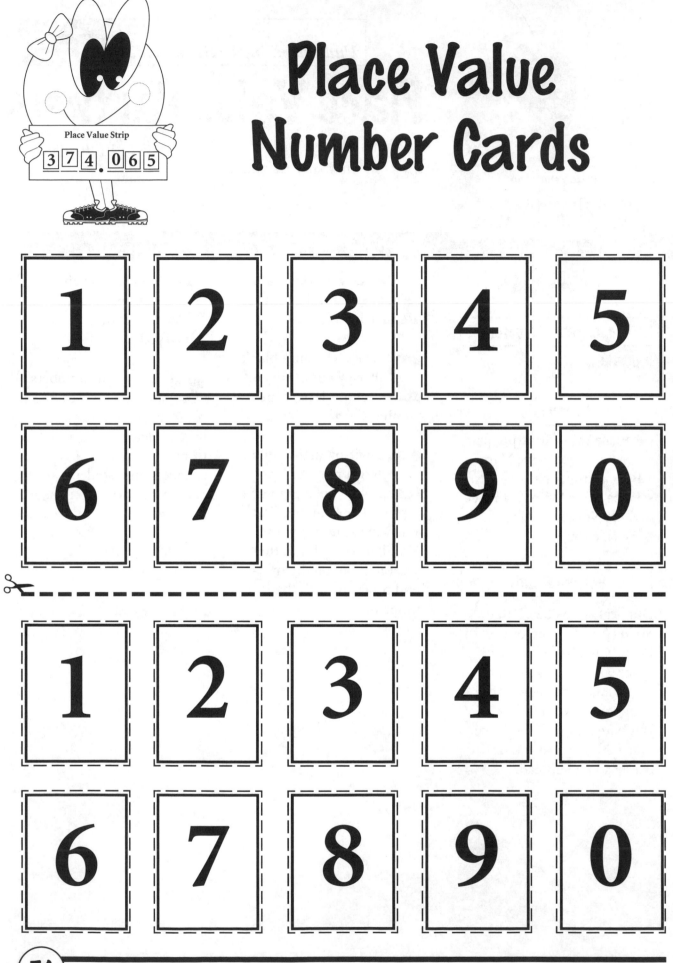

Place Value Strip

3 7 4 . 0 6 5

1 2 3 4 5

6 7 8 9 0

1 2 3 4 5

6 7 8 9 0

 Discovering Decimals by Laura Candler • **Kagan Publishing** • 1 (800) 933-2667 • www.KaganOnline.com

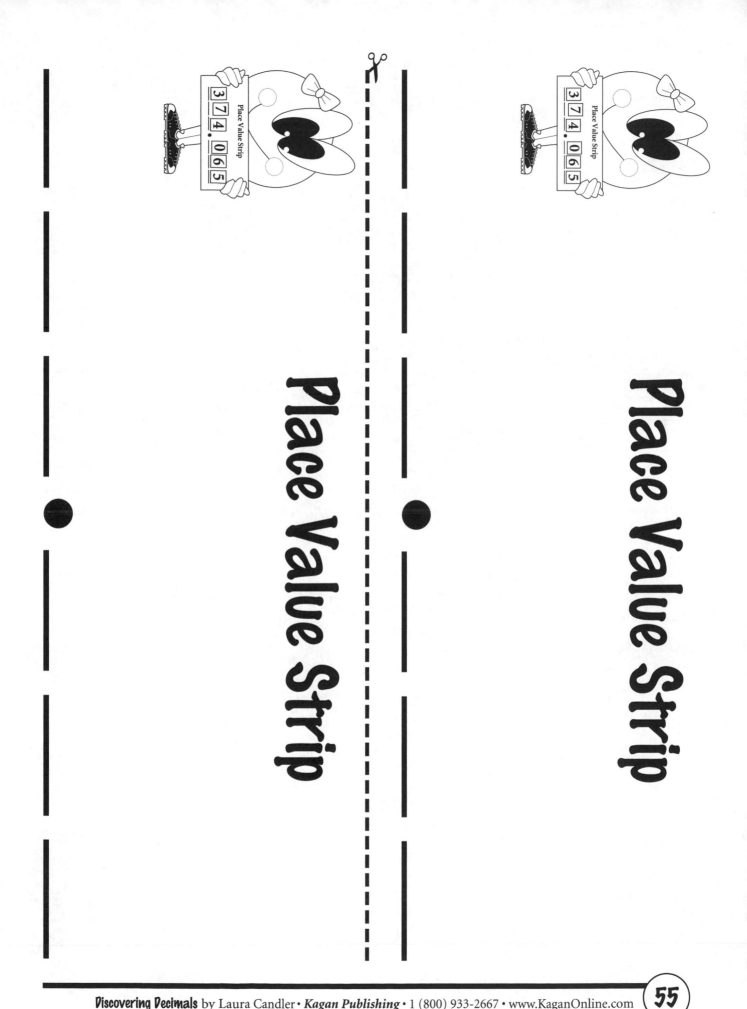

Place Value Strip

Place Value Strip

Place Value Strip

Place Value Strip

3 7 4 . 0 6 5

3 7 4 . 0 6 5

Decimal Match

Decimal Match

3.53

Students mix around the room trading decimal numbers and picture cards. On a signal from the teacher, students stop and find their match.

Cooperative Structure

Mix-N-Match

Materials

- **Decimal Match** worksheets (1 per pair)
- **Crayons, colored pencils, or markers**
- **Transparency of Decimal Match** worksheet (optional)
- **Scissors**

Getting Ready

Make a transparency of the **Decimal Match** (page 58) worksheet to use in demonstrating the lesson setup. Or prepare the **Decimal Match** cards in advance by writing numbers at the top and coloring the corresponding squares on the worksheets. (Prepare one set per pair of students.)

Steps . . .

1 Give each pair of students one **Decimal Match** worksheet, crayons, and scissors.

2 Use the transparency to model the correct procedure for preparing the activity cards. Ask one person to write a decimal number greater than 0 and less than 6 on the upper half of the worksheet. Have the other person color the corresponding squares and sections on the lower half of the worksheet. Students separate the number from the picture by cutting on the dotted line.

3 With each student holding either a picture or a number card, students mix around the room. They trade cards as they mix.

4 After cards are well mixed, announce "Freeze!"

5 Students stop and examine their card.

6 Say "Match!" and have students move about looking for the picture or number that matches their card.

7 Students move to the outside edges of the room when they find their partner.

8 After all students have found their matches, call "Mix" and they play again.

Decimal Match

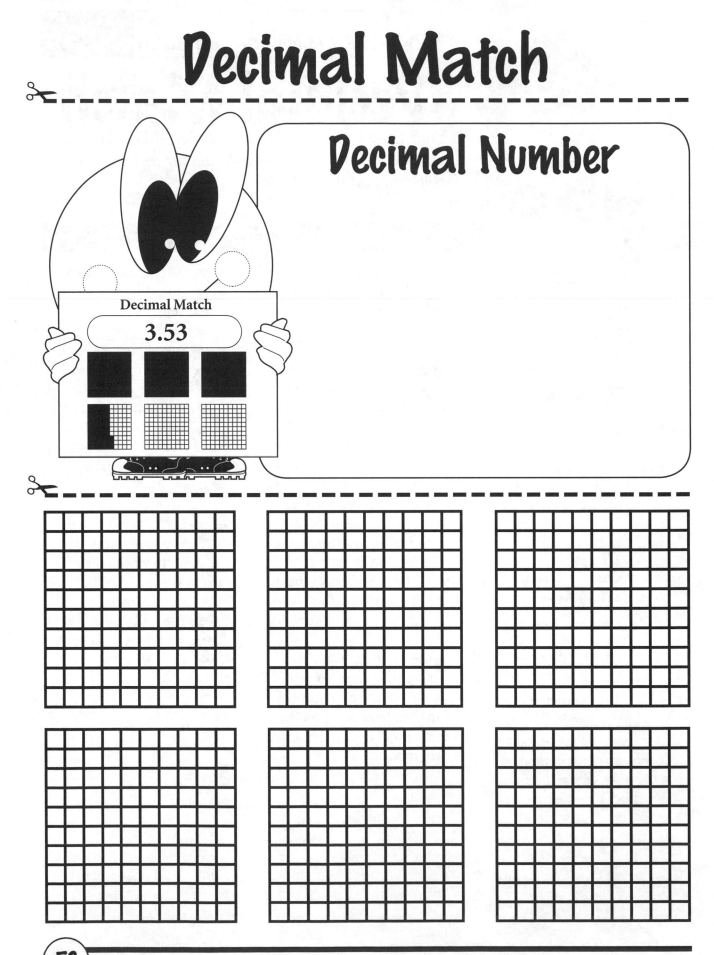

Decimal Number

Decimal Match

3.53

ACTIVITY
1.4

Money Match

Cooperative Structure:

RallyTable

Divide students into pairs and assign each person the role of Partner A or Partner B. Duplicate one **Money Match Placemat** (page 60) for each pair. Give each pair a supply of play money coins, making sure each pair has at least 10 each of the following: pennies, nickels, dimes, and quarters. If play money is not available, duplicate the **Coin Patterns** (page 163).

One person (Partner A) points to a decimal number on the placemat, reads the number aloud, and places the correct number of coins on the decimal. If the answer is correct, Partner B offers praise. If the answer is not correct, the two discuss the problem and place the correct money amount on the mat. Partner B points to a different decimal on the mat, reads it aloud, and properly places the coins. Pairs continue to alternate placing coins on the placemat until it is completely covered.

Placement

0.5

0.1

1.35

Money Match

Place one or more coins on each dollar bill to represent the decimal amount shown.

0.20

0.25

0.01

0.05

0.75

 Discovering Decimals by Laura Candler • **Kagan Publishing** • 1 (800) 933-2667 • www.KaganOnline.com

Cubes	Flats	Rods	Units
	2.39		

Build and Write

Students individually build each decimal with base ten manipulatives and write its word name. Then they compare and discuss their answers.

Steps . . .

1 Give each team a set of **Build and Write Task Cards** to stack face down in the center.

2 Person #1 becomes the first Turn Captain and turns over the top card.

3 All team members individually build the number on their place mats, then write the word name on their response boards.

4 When everyone is ready, the Turn Captain says "Showdown!"

5 Team members simultaneously show their response boards and check each others' Base 10 block arrangements. Discussion follows as needed.

6 Person #2 serves as the new Turn Captain and turns over the next card.

Variations...

• **Expanded Form** - Have students also write the expanded form of the decimal in step 3.

• **Math Journals** - Ask students to draw their Base 10 block arrangements and record the number and word name in their math journals.

• **Learning Center** - If you don't have enough **Base 10 Manipulatives** for the whole class, set up this activity in a learning center.

Cooperative Structure

Showdown

Materials

• **Base 10 Manipulatives** (1 set per person)
• **Base 10 Place Value Mats** (1 per person)
• Individual response boards or paper and pencil
• **Build and Write Task Cards**

Getting Ready

Use the **Build and Write** Task Cards (page 62) blackline to prepare a set of cards for each team. Give each person their own set of **Base 10 Manipulatives** (pages 155-156), including a placemat. Review the terms cube, flat, rod, and unit for the various pieces. Tell students that they will be using the flat to represent one whole.

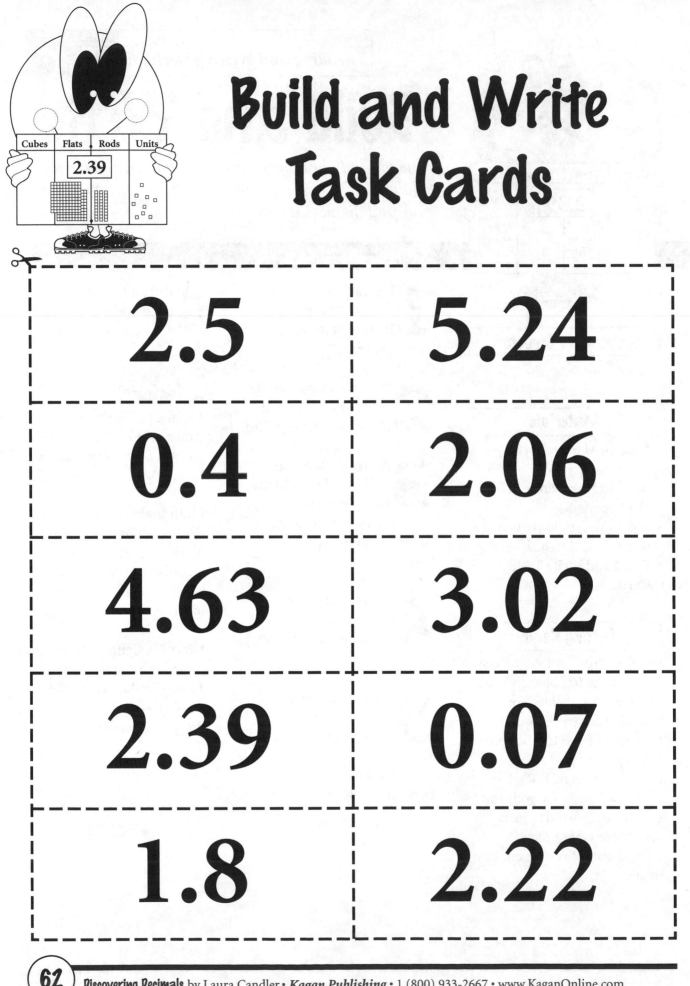

Build and Write Task Cards

2.5	5.24
0.4	2.06
4.63	3.02
2.39	0.07
1.8	2.22

Cubes | Flats | Rods | Units

2.39

Discovering Decimals by Laura Candler • *Kagan Publishing* • 1 (800) 933-2667 • www.KaganOnline.com

One hundred twenty-six and seven tenths

126.7

Decimal Read Around

Students take turns reading decimals aloud.

S t e p s . . .

1 Give each team one set of **Decimal Read Around Cards**. Have them cut the cards apart and place them face down in the center of the team.

2 Designate one person on each team to be the first Reader. This person turns over the top card, shows it to the team, and reads the number aloud.

3 Team members give a thumbs-up if they feel the number was read correctly. If they don't agree, they may offer hints and help. The Reader must try again until he or she is able to correctly read the number.

4 The role of Reader rotates around the team. Each person, in turn, reads one card and waits for team agreement. The activity continues until all 12 cards have been read or the teacher calls time.

Hints...

• **Monitor and Listen** - Move from team to team and listen to individual responses. Stop the class to clarify any problems.

• **Challenge Numbers** - If a team finishes early, have them turn the cards over and write their own challenge numbers on the back. Encourage them to continue with the RoundRobin until the other teams finish.

Cooperative Structure

RoundRobin

Materials

• **Decimal Read Around Cards** (1 copy per team)
• Scissors

Getting Ready

Introduce the proper method for reading decimals aloud prior to this activity. Then duplicate one copy of the **Decimal Read Around Cards** (page 64) for each team. If the decimals on this worksheet are too challenging, use the **Decimal Number Cards** (pages 159-162) to prepare an appropriate set for each team.

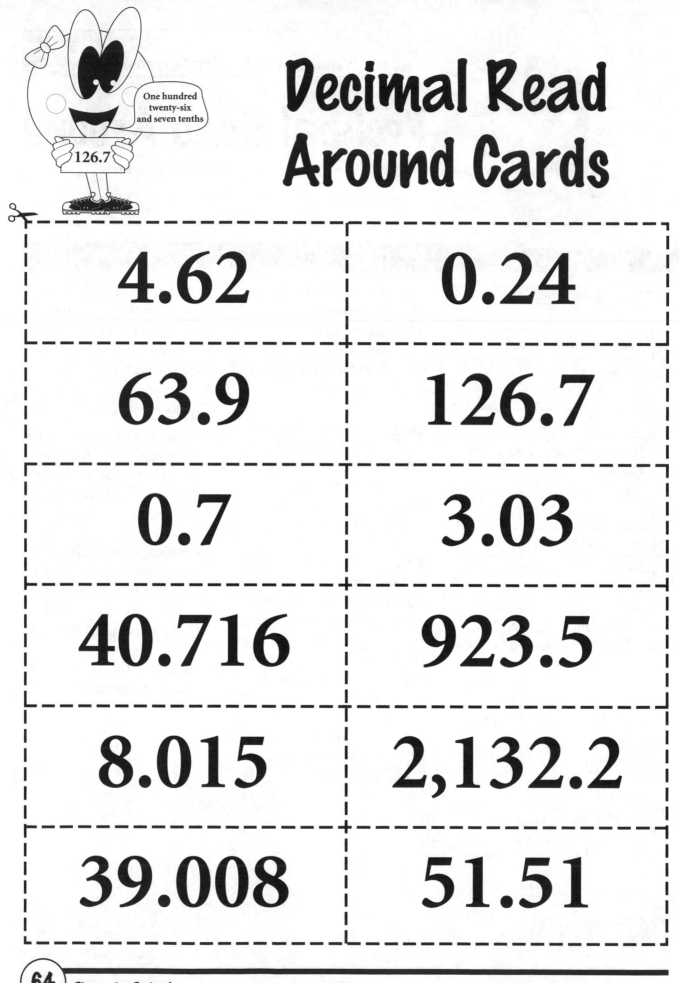

One hundred
twenty-six
and seven tenths

126.7

Decimal Read Around Cards

4.62	0.24
63.9	126.7
0.7	3.03
40.716	923.5
8.015	2,132.2
39.008	51.51

 Discovering Decimals by Laura Candler • *Kagan Publishing* • 1 (800) 933-2667 • www.KaganOnline.com

Forty-two and fifteen hundredths minus...

42.15 - 13.4 - 16.75

Decimal Dozen Count Down

Students take turns reading decimal subtraction problems aloud to a partner who uses a calculator to solve them. Successful calculations lead to the discovery that all answers are "12," an even dozen.

Steps...

Cooperative Structure

RallyTable

Materials

- 1 Calculator per pair
- 1 Set of **Decimal Dozen Count Down** problem cards per pair
- Scissors

Getting Ready

Divide your class into pairs before starting the activity. Review the correct method for reading decimals aloud. Duplicate **Decimal Dozen Count Down** (page 67) for each pair.

1 Give one **Decimal Dozen Count Down** worksheet (page 67) and a calculator to each pair. Have students work together to cut out the cards and stack them face down.

2 Students take turns being the Caller and the Problem Solver. The Caller draws a card and (without showing the card) slowly reads the subtraction problem to the Problem Solver.

3 The Problem Solver enters each number into the calculator as it is read aloud, pressing the subtraction key after the first two numbers and the = key at the end.

4 The Problem Solver shows his or her answer to the Caller. If the answer is "12," the Caller praises the Problem Solver.

5 If the answer is not "12," the Caller places the problem card face up on the table so both can see it. The Caller reads the problem again and watches the Problem Solver enter each number.

6 Players switch roles for the next round. The Problem Solver becomes the Caller and the Caller becomes the new Problem Solver.

7 Students continue switching roles as they practice with the remaining problem cards.

Hints...

- **Secret Pattern** - Don't tell students in advance that all answers will be "12." Instead challenge them to find a pattern to the answers. Monitor the activity to be sure that all pairs discover the pattern after several rounds.

- **Beware of Shortcuts!** - After students have discovered the pattern remind them that the point of the activity is to practice reading and listening to decimals. Some

Decimal Dozen Count Down

Forty-two and
fifteen hundredths
minus...

42.15 - 13.4 - 16.75

students may take advantage of
the "trick" and just enter a "12"
at the end of the problem!

• **Create a Learning Center -**
This activity works well in a
learning center. You can use it
as a part of a Rotation Learning
Center review or as a Learning
Choice Center. Refer to pages
14-15 for more information
about centers.

Decimal Dozen Count Down

16.75

Forty-two and fifteen hundredths minus...

42.15 - 13.4 - 16.75

42.15 - 13.4 - 16.75	85.9 - 49.23 - 24.67
19.54 - 5.03 - 2.51	27.64 - 12.6 - 3.04
98.714 - 86.714	25 - 8.48 - 4.52
43 - 1.964 - 29.036	77.77 - 52.2 - 13.57
34.8 - 0.09 - 22.71	19.67 - 0.371 - 7.299
613.21 - 92.5 - 508.71	16.02 - 0.04 - 3.98

ACTIVITY
2.4

Decimal Writing

Cooperative Structure:
RallyTable

Divide each team into pairs and give each pair one copy of the **RallyTable Decimal Writing** (page 70) worksheet. Students take turns completing the worksheet. One person reads the word name aloud and the other writes the standard form of the decimal on the line. Students switch roles for each problem. For added accountability, let each student write in a different colored pencil. A quick check will show two pencil colors if both students are participating equally.

ACTIVITY
2.5

Paired Decimal Writing

Cooperative Structure:
Pairs Check

Make one copy of the **Paired Decimal Writing** worksheet (page 71) for each pair of students. You can use this worksheet for practice in writing word names, expanded forms, or both. Have them write their names at the top and complete the activity in Pairs Check format according to your specific math instructions.

ACTIVITY
2.6

Wonderful Word Names

Cooperative Structure:
Mix-Freeze-Pair

Each student will need a different Decimal Number Card. To prepare a set of cards for the class, duplicate and cut apart the **Decimal Number Cards** (pages 159-162). Note the difficulty level on each page and use only the cards which are appropriate for your class.

Give each student one **Decimal Number Card**. Have them write the word name for their decimal on the back of the card. Students pair with a teammate to make sure their word names are correct. Announce "mix" and students mill around the room with their card, a piece of paper, and a pencil. After saying "freeze" and "pair," students simultaneously write the word name of the number shown on their partner's card. Pairs check each others' answers and praise or help as needed. When all pairs appear ready, say "mix" and repeat the entire activity as time allows.

Additional
Activities

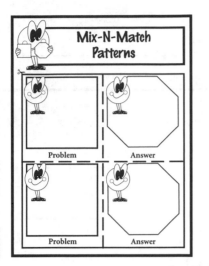

Mix-N-Match Patterns

Problem Answer

Problem Answer

 ACTIVITY
2.7

Decimal Word Match

Cooperative Structure:
Mix-N-Match

Give each team one copy of the blank **Mix-N-Match Patterns** worksheet (page 166) and have them cut out and distribute the four shapes. Ask students with squares to write the standard form of any decimal (such as 34.67) in their square. Have them pair with someone holding an octagon, who will write the word name for the decimal. To check for accuracy, ask teammates to swap cards and make sure each word name correctly matches the standard form of the decimal. Then students take their number or word card with them as they follow the basic Mix-N-Match steps.

ACTIVITY
2.8

Think and Read

Cooperative Structure:
Think-Pair-Share

Seat students in pairs. Write a decimal number on the board. Each person thinks of the correct way to name the decimal, then softly whispers it together with their partner. Call on one person to read the decimal aloud before the class, or have them all say it in unison. Repeat by writing more decimals on the board, increasing the difficulty for each round.

Additional Activities

RallyTable Decimal Writing

ACTIVITY 2.4

Name (A)_____ Name (B)_____

1) Two and fifty-five hundredths _____

2) Eighteen and seven tenths _____

3) Two hundred fifteen and seventy-five hundredths _____

4) Ninety-three hundredths _____

5) Six and fourteen thousandths _____

6) Three hundred twelve and twenty-two hundredths _____

7) Seven and five hundred two thousandths _____

8) Ninety and nineteen thousandths _____

9) Eight tenths _____

10) Forty-one and seven hundredths _____

11) Seventy-two and eighty-three hundredths _____

12) Four thousandths _____

70 *Discovering Decimals* by Laura Candler • *Kagan Publishing* • 1 (800) 933-2667 • www.KaganOnline.com

Paired Decimal Writing

ACTIVITY 2.5

Name _____   Name _____

A   B

1) **8.67**	2) **23.9**
3) **90.26**	4) **0.005**
5) **128.4**	6) **400.39**
7) **14.02**	8) **6.893**
9) **3.0092**	10) **605.8**
11) **0.78**	12) **45.0673**

Build and Compare

Students compare two decimals by building them with Base 10 manipulatives.

Cubes	Flats	Rods	Units

2.31
< 2.4

Cooperative Structure

Think-Pair-Share

Materials

• **Place Value Mats**
  (1 per pair)
• **Base 10 Manipulatives**
  (1 set per pair)
• Paper and pencil

Getting Ready

Divide your students into pairs and make sure each pair has a set of **Base 10 Manipulatives** (pages 155-156). (Each set needs at least 2 cubes, 9 flats, 9 rods, and 9 units.) Prepare a **Place Value Mat** (page 154) for each pair according to the directions.

Steps . . .

1 Write two decimal numbers on the board (such as 2.31 and 2.4). Use the **Build and Compare** list at right or write your own.

2 Ask students to think individually about which number is larger and jot that one down.

3 Demonstrate how to use the manipulatives and Place Value Mat. Build the first number (2.31) on the top row and the second number (2.4) on the bottom row. After you demonstrate, Partner A builds the first number and Partner B builds the second on the **Place Value Mat** between them.

4 Pairs discuss which number is larger according to the Base 10 block arrangement.

Build and Compare

23.6 or 23.72
4.68 or 4.5
9.2 or 9.02
16.04 or 16.9
0.76 or 1.3
21.8 or 23.4
17.9 or 17.48

5 Call on students to explain which number is larger and why.

6 Placemats are cleared. Continue writing decimal pairs on the board. For each pair of numbers, repeat the steps above.

Decimal War

Students play a version of the classic card game "War," using decimals cards instead of regular playing cards. In each round, the person with the largest decimal number captures the other card or cards.

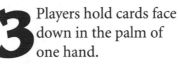

S t e p s . . .

Cooperative Structure

Play-N-Switch

Materials

- **Decimal War Cards**
  (1 set per pair)
- Scissors for each student

Getting Ready

Duplicate the **Decimal War Cards** (pages 77-79) on card stock or construction paper if possible. You'll need all three pages to make each deck, and you'll need one deck for each pair of students.

Ask if students have ever played the card game "War." If so, have someone explain the basic rules (see steps below). Tell them that Decimal War is played the same way except that **Decimal War Cards** are used and the winner of each round is the person with the largest decimal. Make sure students have had practice comparing decimals before playing the game.

1 Give each pair the three pages of **Decimal War Cards**. Have them cut out all cards and place the cards face down between them.

2 One person shuffles the deck and deals both players an equal number of cards.

3 Players hold cards face down in the palm of one hand.

4 Players remove the top card from their deck and place it face up on the table in front of them.

5 The player whose card has the higher value keeps both cards. The winner of that round must explain why his or her card is larger.

6 If both cards have the same value, "war" is declared. Both players place three cards face down on the table as they say, "I declare war!" They turn the fourth card face up and compare numbers. The player whose card has the higher value keeps all the cards for that round.

7 Play continues until one person wins all the cards or until the time is up. If time is called, the winner is the player with the most cards.

8 Players discuss strategies and switch partners.

Hints...

- **Heterogeneous Pairing** - Don't pair two students who are having difficulty with comparing decimals. Instead, pair students who have mastered the skill with those who haven't. Encourage the stronger students to help their partners, even if it means losing a card to their opponent.

Decimal War

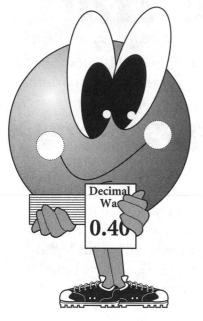

- **Create a Learning Center -** This activity makes an excellent learning center. You can use it as a part of a Rotation Learning Center review or set it up as a Learning Choice Center. Refer to pages 14-15 for more information about centers.

- **Monitor Carefully -** Make sure the winners for each round explain why they know their decimal is the larger of the two. Also, watch for stronger students who might take advantage of a weaker student's lack of skills.

Decimal War Cards

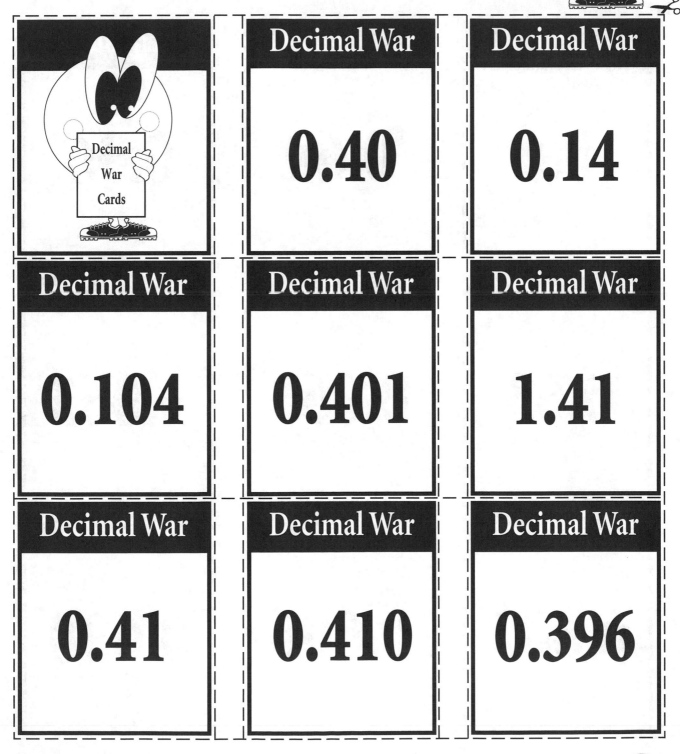

	Decimal War	Decimal War
Decimal War Cards	**0.40**	**0.14**
Decimal War	Decimal War	Decimal War
0.104	**0.401**	**1.41**
Decimal War	Decimal War	Decimal War
0.41	**0.410**	**0.396**

Decimal War Cards

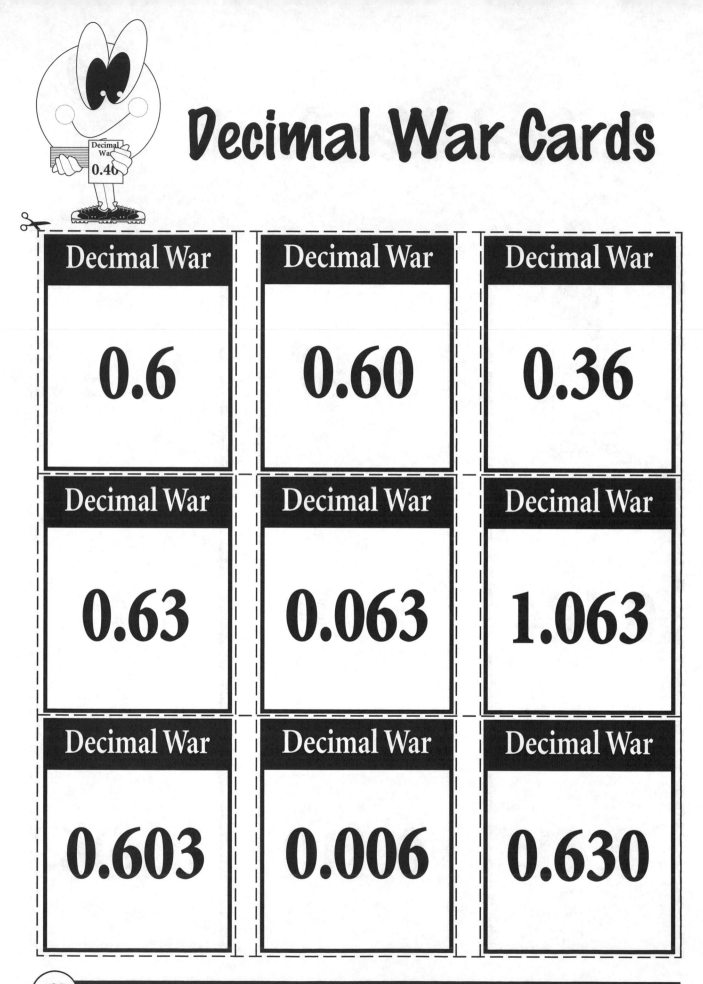

Decimal War	Decimal War	Decimal War
0.6	**0.60**	**0.36**
0.63	**0.063**	**1.063**
0.603	**0.006**	**0.630**

 Discovering Decimals by Laura Candler • *Kagan Publishing* • 1 (800) 933-2667 • www.KaganOnline.com

Decimal War Cards

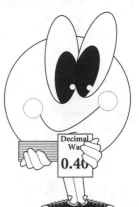

Decimal War	Decimal War	Decimal War
0.9	**0.96**	**0.096**
Decimal War	Decimal War	Decimal War
0.690	**1.9**	**1.3**
Decimal War	Decimal War	Decimal War
1.366	**1.936**	**0.4**

0.002
0.08
0.285
0.43
0.52
0.81
0.83
0.955

What's The Order?

Students in pairs take turns placing decimal numbers as they arrange them in sequential order. Then they compare their sequence with another pair of students.

Steps...

1 Give each pair Set 1 only of the **What's the Order?** worksheet. If the cards have not been cut apart, ask the students to separate them. Have them mix up the cards and deal them out so that each person has the same number.

2 Ask Partner A to place one card face up between the two students.

3 Tell students that they will be working with their partner to put the rest of the decimals in order from least (at the top) to greatest (at the bottom). Partner B places a card either above or below the first card according to its proper sequence.

4 Partner A places another card in sequence. If the other cards have to be moved to fit in the new card, Partner A must ask permission before moving them.

5 Students continue to take turns placing and adjusting cards until all cards have been properly sequenced.

6 When both pairs on a team have finished, they compare their solutions. They celebrate correct answers or discuss and correct any problems.

7 All team members raise their hands to signal that they are finished and ready to be checked. If they have sequenced Set 1 correctly, give them Set 2 to complete.

Hints...

- **Sponge Activity** - Give students index cards and let them make up their own **What's the Order?** number cards. Have them make two sets so that they can follow the same sequence of steps as above.

Cooperative Structure

Pairs Compare

Materials

- **What's the Order?** worksheets (1 per pair)
- Scissors

Getting Ready

Divide each team into pairs. Designate one person in each pair as Partner A and the other as Partner B. Prepare one copy of the **What's the Order?** worksheet (page 82) for each pair. Cut the worksheet down the center of the page so that you can distribute the two sets of number cards separately. (This will keep students from mixing the two sets together by mistake.)

Briefly review a variety of methods for comparing and ordering decimals.

What's The Order?

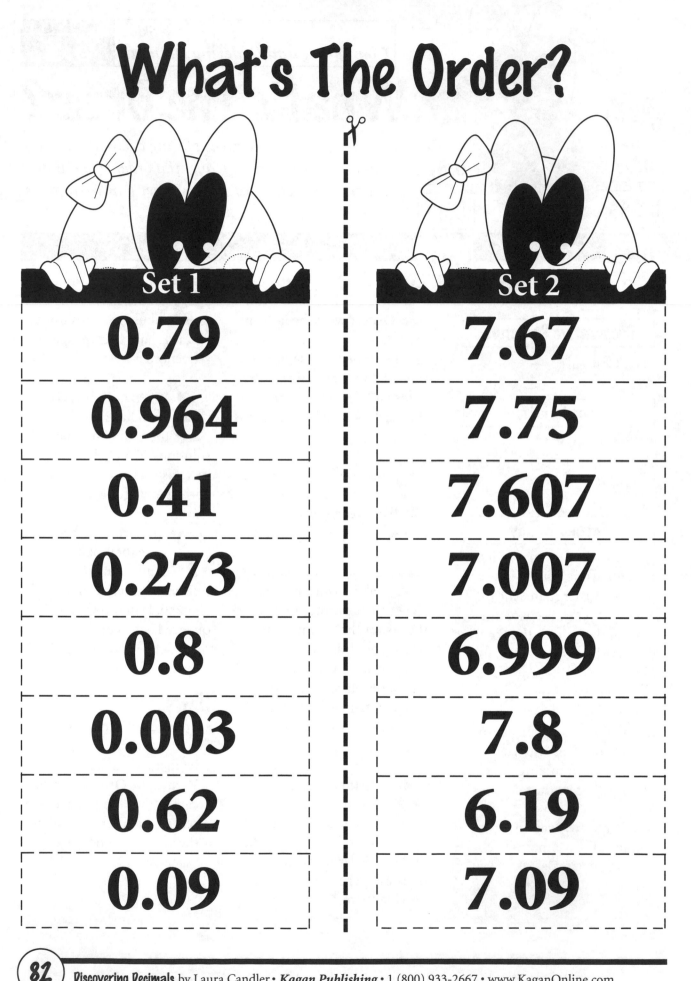

Set 1	Set 2
0.79	**7.67**
0.964	**7.75**
0.41	**7.607**
0.273	**7.007**
0.8	**6.999**
0.003	**7.8**
0.62	**6.19**
0.09	**7.09**

I'm the Greatest!

Students in teams use knowledge of place value concepts and attempt to write the largest number.

I'm the Greatest!

I'm the Greatest!

9 7 5 . 3 4 1

Cooperative Structure

RoundTable

Materials

- Deck of playing cards or **Place Value Number Cards** (1 per team)
- **I'm the Greatest** worksheet (1 or more per person)
- Crayons (1 per person)

Getting Ready

A deck of playing cards works well for this activity, but if you don't have a deck for each team you can create sets of number cards by duplicating the **Place Value Number Cards** (page 54) on heavy paper. If you do have a deck of playing cards for each team, remove the Kings and Queens. Tell students that Aces are ones and Jacks are zeros.

Steps...

1 Give each team a deck of at least 20 cards numbered 0 - 9. Have them shuffle the cards and place them face down in the center of the team. Give each team member one **I'm the Greatest** worksheet and a crayon. Number students off from 1 to 4.

2 Explain that the object of the activity is to write the largest number possible. Students will start in the section marked "Round 1" on their **I'm the Greatest** worksheet.

3 Person #1 on each team becomes the first Number Reader. He or she begins by turning over the top number card and reading it aloud. Using a crayon, everyone writes the number in one of the blanks under Round 1. *Once a number has been written, it can not be changed.*

4 Person #2 turns over the next card and reads it aloud. Everyone writes the number in any spot as before. Continue rotating the role of Number Reader until all blanks for Round 1 have been filled.

5 Team members compare their final numbers. The person with the greatest number says "I'm the Greatest!" and reads his or her number correctly to the team.

6 Students congratulate the winner and discuss playing strategies while one team member reshuffles the cards.

7 The remaining rounds are played in the same way as Round 1.

Hints...

- **Cooperation vs. Competition** - Remind students that the purpose of the game is to work on decimal skills, not just to win. You can keep the competitive aspects low key by not offering prizes and other tangible rewards to the "winners."

I'm The Greatest!

I'm the Greatest!

I'm the Greatest!

9 7 5 . 3 4 1

- **Reusable Worksheets** - You can save paper by laminating your **I'm The Greatest** worksheets prior to the lesson and letting students write on them with overhead pens.

- **Create a Learning Center** - This activity makes an excellent learning center. You can use it as a part of a Rotation Learning Center review or set it up as a Learning Choice Center. Refer to pages 14-15 for more information about centers.

- **Justifying Answers** - Make sure students discuss why a particular number is greater than the others. Monitor the activity by circulating and asking the winner of each round to explain why his or her answer is the "greatest."

I'm The Greatest!

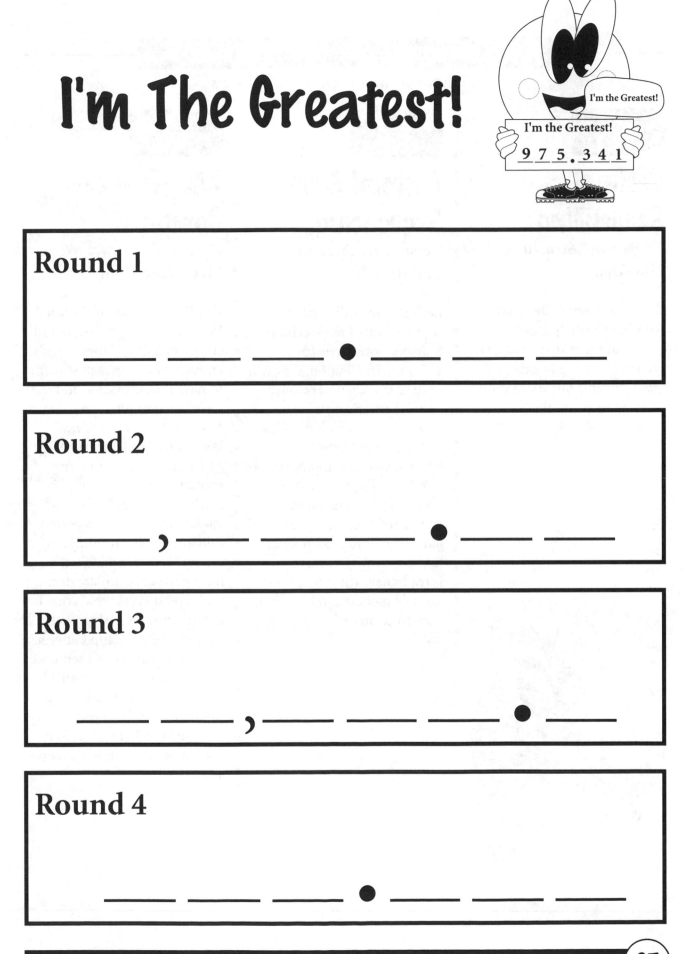

I'm the Greatest!

I'm the Greatest!

9 7 5 . 3 4 1

Round 1

___ ___ ___ • ___ ___ ___

Round 2

___ , ___ ___ ___ • ___ ___

Round 3

___ ___ , ___ ___ ___ • ___

Round 4

___ ___ ___ • ___ ___ ___

ACTIVITY
3.5

Decimal Sequencing

Cooperative Structure:
Line-Ups

Duplicate a set of **Decimal Number Cards** (pages 159-162). Cut them apart and give each student one number. Have students line up in the order of their numbers.

ACTIVITY
3.6

Decimal Square Sequencing

Cooperative Structure:
Line-Ups

Each student will need one copy of each of the **Decimal Squares** worksheets (pages 157-158). In addition, they will need scissors, glue, crayons, and a sheet of construction paper. Have each person illustrate a decimal between 0 and 6 by coloring the appropriate numbers of squares and sections. Ask them to cut out their completed decimal squares and glue them onto the construction paper. When everyone is ready, have them take their decimal models and line up in numerical order.

ACTIVITY
3.7

Mix-Freeze-Compare

Cooperative Structure:
Mix-Freeze-Pair

Duplicate one set of **Decimal War Cards** (pages 77-79) and cut them apart. If there aren't enough cards for each student to have one, duplicate and cut apart an additional set. Give each student one **Decimal War Card**. Students pair with a team member to practice pronouncing the decimal correctly. Announce "Mix" and students take their cards and mill around the room. After saying "Freeze" and "Pair," have partners compare decimals and discuss which one is greater in value. Ask pairs to state the relationship between the two numbers in a sentence. For example, "Seven tenths is greater than thirty-four hundredths." Continue prompting students to Mix, Freeze, Pair, and compare decimals as time allows.

Additional Activities

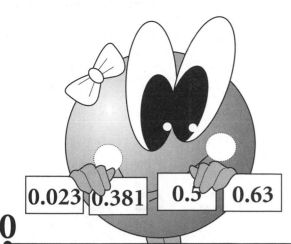

0.023 0.381   0.5   0.63

0 —————————————————————————— 1

Zero To One

Students holding number signs find their correct placement on a number line.

Steps...

1 Give each student one **Zero to One Decimal Card**, a piece of paper or index card, a crayon, and a clothespin or paper clip.

2 Tell students to write their number large on the index card or paper.

3 When everyone is ready, have them line up along the number line where they believe their number to be. Students are encouraged to help each other and discuss their relative locations.

4 Ask each person to clip their number to the number line in its correct location.

5 Have students return to their seats and examine all the numbers on the number line.

6 Move down the number line and point to each number indi-vidually. Ask students to give a "thumbs up" or "thumbs down" sign to show agreement or disagreement with the position of each number.

7 If a number is incorrectly placed, let teams discuss its correct location. Call on a student to move the number and explain why the number should occupy a different position.

Hints...

- **Mark Tenths** - If students have trouble with this activity, divide the string into tenths and mark each section with a small sign or piece of tape.

- **Additional Practice** - Change the labels on the ends of the string to 10 and 15. Have students take a new slip of paper and write a decimal number between 10 and 15. Repeat the Line-Up using the new numbers.

Cooperative Structure

Line-Ups

Materials

- Yarn or string
- Paper clips
- 6" x 9" sheets of construc-tion paper or large index cards
- **Zero to One Decimal Cards** (1 copy for the class)
- Crayons or markers

Getting Ready

Using the backs of two chairs, string a length of yarn across the classroom about waist-high. Label one end "0" and the other end "1." Cut apart the **Zero to One Decimal Cards** (page 88) so that you have one for each student.

Zero To One Decimal Cards

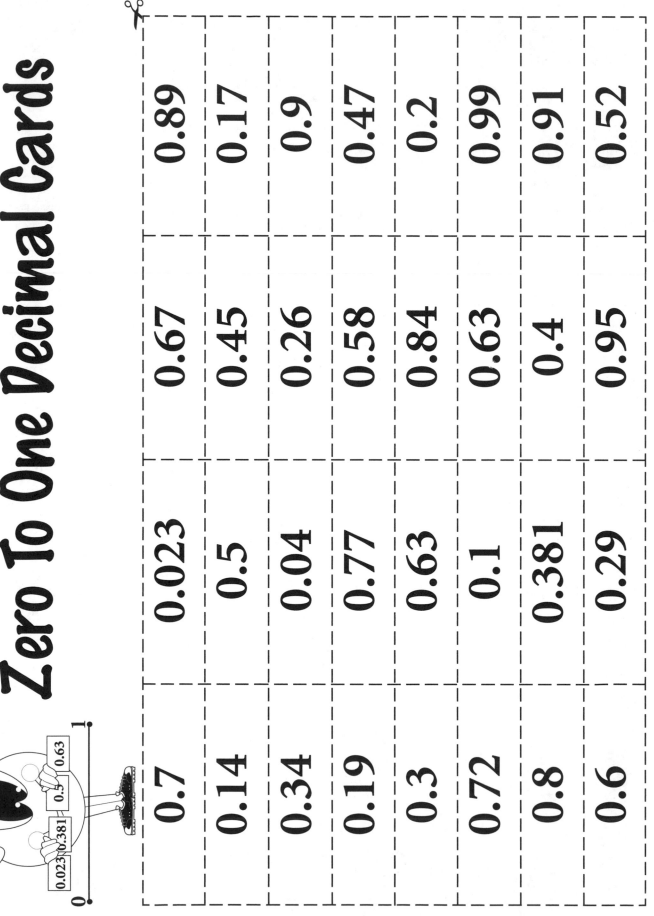

0.7	0.023	0.67	0.89
0.14	0.5	0.45	0.17
0.34	0.04	0.26	0.9
0.19	0.77	0.58	0.47
0.3	0.63	0.84	0.2
0.72	0.1	0.63	0.99
0.8	0.381	0.4	0.91
0.6	0.29	0.95	0.52

 Discovering Decimals by Laura Candler • *Kagan Publishing* • 1 (800) 933-2667 • www.KaganOnline.com

ACTIVITY 4.2

Thinking About Number Lines

Cooperative Structure:
Think-Pair-Share

Give each pair of students a copy of the **Thinking About Number Lines** worksheet (page 90) to place between them. Place a transparency of the same sheet on the overhead. Call out a decimal such as 15.8 and have students think about where it would be located. Then have them point to the location on the number line and discuss their answers with their partner. Finally, project the number line on the screen and have several people come forward and show where they think the correct placement is. Continue these steps with different numbers.

ACTIVITY 4.3

Number Line Star Search

Cooperative Structure:
Pairs Compare

Give each pair one copy of the **Number Line Star Search** worksheet (page 91). Ask students to use different colored pencils (or a pencil and a pen) for accountability. Have students take turns writing the decimals in the stars below the correct points on the number lines. When each pair is finished, tell them to do a Pairs Compare with their teammates.

Additional Activities

Thinking About Number Lines

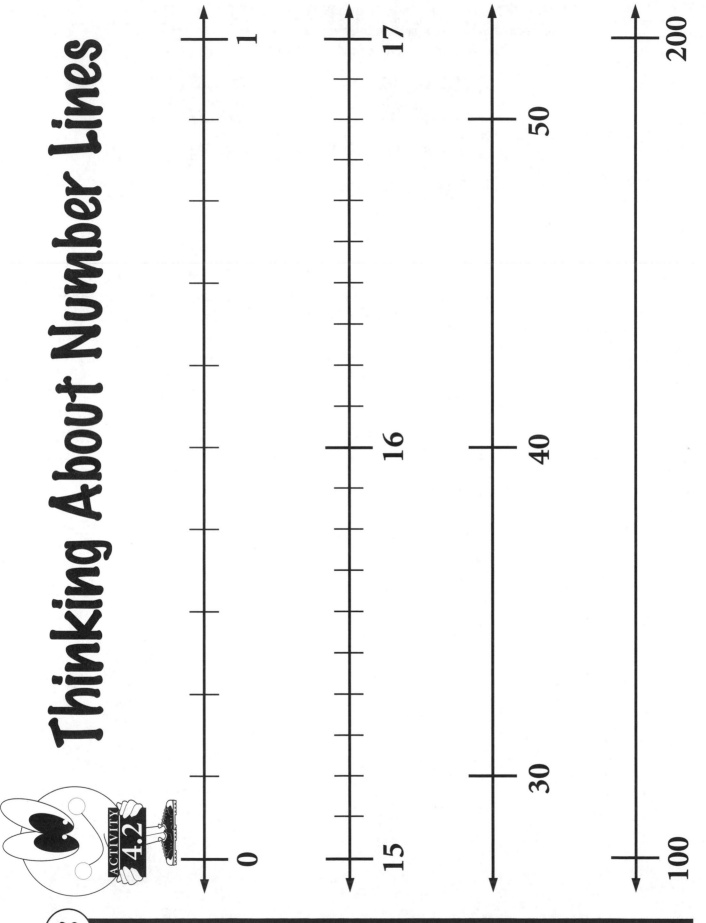

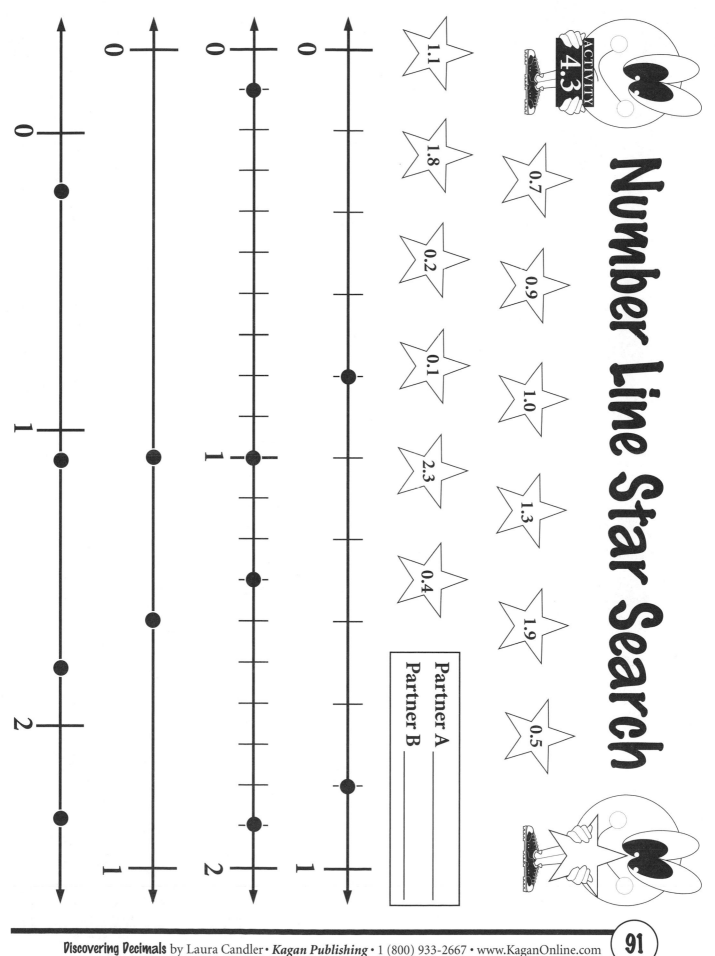

Number Line Star Search

☆ 1.1 ☆ 1.8 ☆ 0.2 ☆ 0.1 ☆ 2.3 ☆ 0.4

☆ 0.7 ☆ 0.9 ☆ 1.0 ☆ 1.3 ☆ 1.9 ☆ 0.5

Partner A _____
Partner B _____

Discovering Decimals by Laura Candler • *Kagan Publishing* • 1 (800) 933-2667 • www.KaganOnline.com

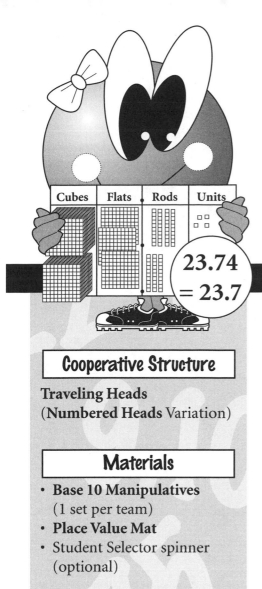

Cubes | Flats | Rods | Units

23.74 = 23.7

Cooperative Structure

Traveling Heads
(**Numbered Heads** Variation)

Materials

- **Base 10 Manipulatives**
  (1 set per team)
- **Place Value Mat**
- Student Selector spinner
  (optional)

Getting Ready

Prepare a **Place Value Mat** for each team by following the directions on page 154. If you don't have **Base 10 Manipulatives**, use the patterns on pages 155-156 to create one set for each team. Each set should have at least 3 cubes, 10 flats, 10 rods, and 10 units.

Travel-A-Round

Team members build a decimal with base 10 manipulatives and round the number to the place named. Then one member travels to a new team to share the answer.

Steps...

1 Number students off 1 to 4. Give each team a set of manipulatives and a **Place Value Mat**. Divide **Base 10 Manipulatives** among team members as follows: #1 - cubes, #2 - units, #3 - rods, #4 - units.

2 Write a decimal on the overhead, such as 23.74. (See **Travel-A-Round** numbers at right.) Have students build it in RoundTable fashion on the **Place Value Mat**. Remind students that cubes are tens, flats are ones, rods are tenths, and units are hundredths.

3 Teacher gives directions for rounding such as "Round to the nearest tenth." All team members point to the place named on the **Place Value Mat** (the 7 rods in the previous example).

4 Students look to the right of the place named and decide if the number of items *is 5 or higher*. If so, they round the number up by adding one to

Travel-A-Round Numbers
23.74
4.65
3.46
16.76
13.27
.98
9.33
7.04

the place named and removing the manipulatives to the right.

5 If the number in that place is less than five, the team removes the manipulatives to the right of that place to show the answer. In the example above, students would remove the four units.

6 Randomly call a number from 1 to 4, using a spinner if possible. The person writes down the number in its rounded form. (For example, 23.7 in the previous example.)

Travel-A-Around

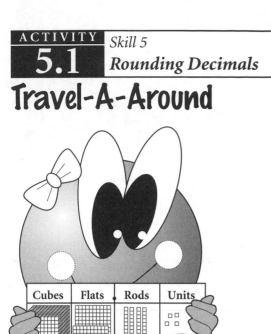

Cubes	Flats	Rods	Units

23.74 = 23.7

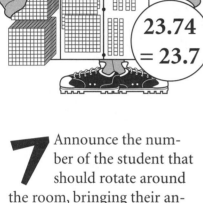

7 Announce the number of the student that should rotate around the room, bringing their answer slip and the number of teams to travel. After arriving at the new team, the student says the correct answer and checks the new team's **Place Value Mat**. If the number and/or **Base 10 Manipulatives** arrangement is different, the team discusses the problem further.

8 Repeat the steps using different decimals and rounding to different places.

Round to the Nearest Hundredth

67.86

Round About

Students mix around the room, pairing up to practice rounding decimals.

Cooperative Structure

Mix-Freeze-Pair

Materials

· 1 **Round About Card** per person
· Scrap paper and a pencil for each person

Getting Ready

Duplicate 7 or 8 sets of **Round About Cards** (page 96) for the class. Write in decimal numbers which are appropriate for students to practice rounding to the place named. Cut the cards apart so that each student will have one card.

Steps . . .

1 Give each person one prepared **Round About Card**. Have them round off the number to the place named and write the answer on the back.

2 Students pair with a partner to make sure they have rounded the number correctly.

3 Announce "Mix" and students mill around the room. Each person brings their **Round About Card**, a piece of paper, and a pencil.

4 Say "Freeze" and "Pair." Students find a partner and simultaneously round each others' decimals according to the place named. Students use their scrap paper to write the answer.

5 Pairs check each others' answers and praise or help as needed.

6 When everyone is ready, announce "Mix!" and repeat the entire activity as time allows.

Round About Cards

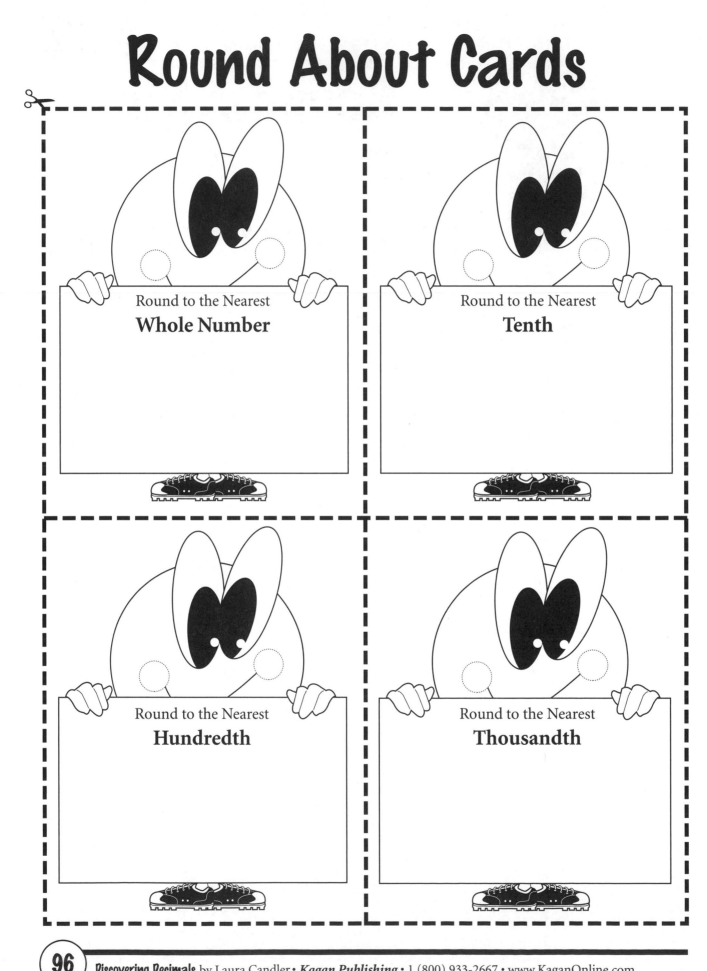

Round to the Nearest
Whole Number

Round to the Nearest
Tenth

Round to the Nearest
Hundredth

Round to the Nearest
Thousandth

Discovering Decimals by Laura Candler • *Kagan Publishing* • 1 (800) 933-2667 • www.KaganOnline.com

ACTIVITY 5.3

Round Around

Cooperative Structure:
RoundRobin

To prepare manipulatives for this activity, make five copies of the **Round About Cards** (page 96). On each card, write a number that can be rounded to the place named. Duplicate a set of cards for each team. Have students cut the cards apart and place them face down in the center of the team. Students take turns flipping over a card, showing it to the team, reading it aloud, and rounding it to the place named.

ACTIVITY 5.4

Rounding Showdown

Cooperative Structure:
Showdown

Use the **Round About Cards** blackline (page 96) to prepare a set of task cards for rounding decimals. Place a set of **Round About Cards** face down in the center of each team, and have the first Turn Captain turn over the top card. Everyone rounds the decimal to the place named, then compares and checks answers. The Turn Captain records the team answer on the card for the teacher to check later.

Additional Activities

Spend It!

Students estimate the number of items that can be bought with a certain amount of money. The person with the closest estimate "wins."

Cooperative Structure

Play-N-Switch

Materials

- **Spend It** game board (1 per pair)
- Two different colored markers (beans, bingo chips, play money, paper clips, etc.)
- Calculators (1 per person)

Getting Ready

Divide your students into pairs. Review estimation of sums, especially with regard to money. Duplicate one **Spend It!** game board (page100) for each pair.

Steps...

1 Give each pair one **Spend It** game board (page 100), two different colored markers, and one calculator. Students place the game board between them. For each round, they try to spend a specific amount of money by estimating the total cost of selected items. The target amounts for each round are found along the bottom of the game board. The amount for Round 1 is $10.

2 To "buy" items, players take turns placing game markers on individual items on the game board. They stop when they believe they have reached the target amount without going over. Students may place as many or as few markers as they want, but they must take turns putting them on the gameboard.

3 When both players have finished "buying" items, they use their calculators to check one person's exact total and then the other's. The person who gets closest to the target number without going over is declared the winner.

4 Students congratulate each other and discuss winning strategies.

5 Students find two other classmates who have also finished and switch partners. They use the target number for Round 2 for the new game. If students finish all 5 rounds, they start over using the target number for Round 1.

Hints...

- **Reward Cooperation** - Instead of rewarding winners, call attention to students who are cooperating and playing fair.

- **Teacher Plays** - Occasionally join in and play a game yourself, especially if you have an odd number of students. Students become excited about math games when they see their teacher enthusiastically involved.

Spend It!

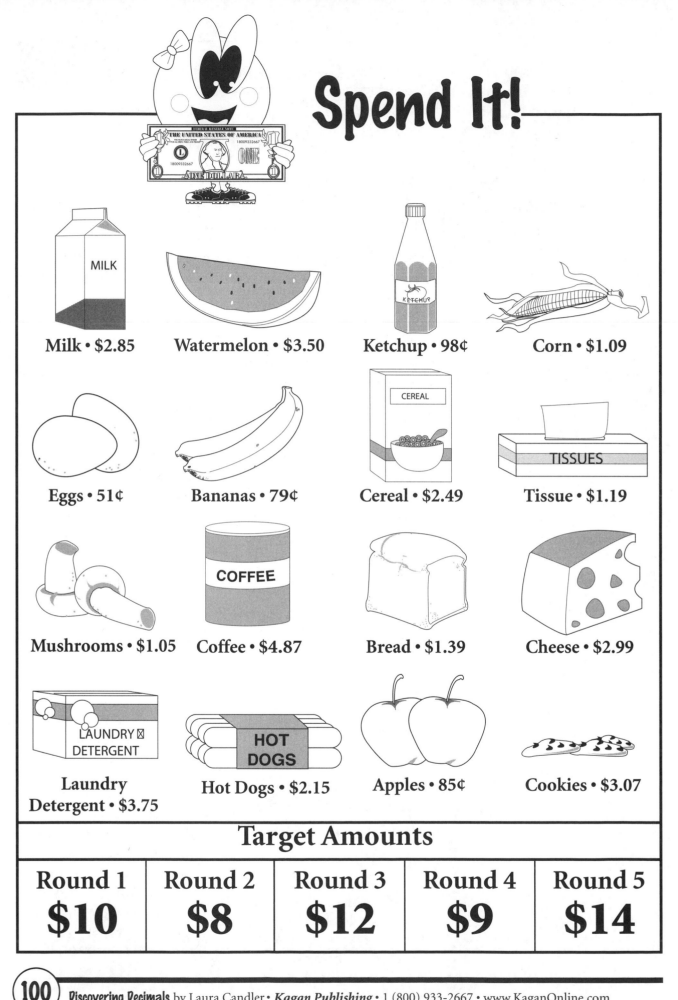

Milk • $2.85

Watermelon • $3.50

Ketchup • 98¢

Corn • $1.09

Eggs • 51¢

Bananas • 79¢

Cereal • $2.49

Tissue • $1.19

Mushrooms • $1.05

Coffee • $4.87

Bread • $1.39

Cheese • $2.99

Laundry Detergent • $3.75

Hot Dogs • $2.15

Apples • 85¢

Cookies • $3.07

Target Amounts

Round 1	Round 2	Round 3	Round 4	Round 5
$10	$8	$12	$9	$14

ACTIVITY 6.2

Estimation Check

Cooperative Structure:
Pairs Check

Write a variety of computation problems in the boxes of a blank **Pairs Check Form** (page 165). Instead of having students find the exact answers, have them estimate the solutions and explain their estimation methods to their partner and team.

ACTIVITY 6.3

Estimation Match

Cooperative Structure:
Mix-N-Match

Prepare problem and answer cards in advance or have the students use the blank **Mix-N-**Match Patterns (page 166) to prepare the cards before the activity. Write one decimal problem (addition and/or subtraction) on each square. Write each problem's estimated answer on the corresponding octagon. Cut apart the cards and follow the basic Mix-N-Match directions.

ACTIVITY 6.4

Estimate Around

Cooperative Structure:
RoundRobin

Use index cards to prepare a set of estimation problems. Stack the problems face down in the center of the team. Have each student, in turn, flip over the top card, read the problem aloud, and estimate the answer using mental math. Encourage students to talk through the steps they use. For example, "First I round 12.81 to 13. Then I round 21.3 to 21. Finally I add 13 and 21 to get 34."

ACTIVITY 6.5

Buzzing for Sums and Differences

Cooperative Structure:
Play-N-Switch

Follow the directions for Buzzing for Products (pages 109-110), but have students add or subtract the numbers on the bees instead of multiplying them.

Additional Activities

It All Adds Up

Students in pairs add decimals using Base 10 manipulatives.

Cubes	Flats	Rods	Units

3.45
+ 2.34
= 5.79

Cooperative Structure

RallyTable

Materials

- **Place Value Mats**
  (1 per pair)
- **Base 10 Manipulatives**
  (1 set per pair)
- **Paper and pencil**

Getting Ready

Divide your students into pairs and designate Partners A and B. Make sure each pair has a set of **Base 10 Manipulatives** (pages 155-156). Each set needs at least 2 cubes, 9 flats, 9 rods, and 9 units. Prepare a **Place Value Mat** for each pair according to the directions on page 154.

Steps...

1 Give each pair a **Place Value Mat** and a set of **Base 10 Manipulatives** to share. Choose two numbers to add that don't involve regrouping, such as 3.45 and 2.34. Write the numbers on the board.

2 Demonstrate how to build the first number on the **Place Value Mat**. Ask Partner A to put 3 flats, 4 rods, and 5 units in their correct locations in the top row only.

3 Next, have Partner B build the second decimal in the bottom row on the mat.

4 Ask students to discuss with their partner how they could add the two numbers. Lead them to see that they can move all their units into one pile, all their rods into another, and their flats into a third. The new number is the sum of both addends.

5 Ask students to clear their **Place Value Mats**. Give them a pair of addends which requires regrouping, such as 7.65 and 4.87. Ask Partner B to build the first number and Partner A to build the second one.

6 This time, lead students through the steps of regrouping. First one person adds the units. If there are more than 9, he or she regroups using rods. Next, the other person add rods, regrouping as needed. The first person adds flats, regrouping with cubes if needed. Make sure students are taking turns as they handle the manipulatives.

Hints...

- **Decimal Alignment** - This activity is perfect for demonstrating the need to line up decimals in addition (and subtraction). Use numbers such as 2.67 and 35.8 to show students why decimal alignment is so important.

It All Adds Up

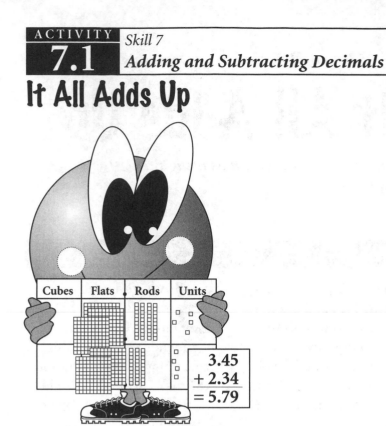

Cubes	Flats	Rods	Units

3.45
+ 2.34
= 5.79

- **Linking Concrete and Abstract Concepts** - After having students solve several addition problems using **Base 10 Manipulatives**, start writing the addition problem on the board. Solve the problem step-by-step on the board as students solve it with their manipulatives. Later in the lesson, have them solve problems by drawing Base 10 block illustrations. Finally, teach them to add without manipulatives.

Pairs Check Sums and Differences

A	B
221.45	87.95
+ 562.38	+ 72.36
= 783.83	= 160.31

Pairs Check Sums and Differences

Students work in pairs, taking turns to solve simple computation problems. After completing each row of problems, pairs check answers with teammates.

S t e p s . . .

1 Give each pair one **Pairs Check Sums and Differences** worksheet (page 106). Partner A works the first problem in the "A" column. He or she lines the numbers up in the space provided and talks through the steps. Partner B coaches and praises.

2 Partner B works the first problem in the "B" column, talking through the steps. Partner A coaches and praises.

3 When both pairs are ready, all four team members check and discuss answers. They may use a calculator to verify their results.

4 The team celebrates the correct answer and places a check in the first box on their worksheets.

5 Students repeat the steps above to finish the worksheet.

Cooperative Structure

Pairs Check

Materials

• **Pairs Check Sums and Differences** worksheet (1 per pair)
• Calculators, 1 per team (optional)

Getting Ready

Use the overhead projector or chalkboard to introduce students to decimal addition and subtraction. Make sure they understand how and why the decimal points must be lined up in order to solve the problems.

Pairs Check Sums and Differences

(A) Name _____	(B) Name _____	
1) 234.65 + 581.54	2) 92.84 + 73.28	☐
3) 59.245 - 32.482	4) 837.26 - 126.47	☐
5) 93.4 + 6.57	6) 5.643 + 27.9	☐
7) 705.46 - 43.8	8) 25.351 + 7.08	☐
9) 39.7 + 4.893	10) 437.45 - 291.8	☐
11) 27.9 - 15.345	12) 56 + 37.84	☐

 Discovering Decimals by Laura Candler • *Kagan Publishing* • 1 (800) 933-2667 • www.KaganOnline.com

ACTIVITY 7.3

Take It Away

Cooperative Structure:
RallyTable

Take It Away is an excellent way to introduce students to decimal subtraction. The steps of Take It Away are almost exactly like **It All Adds Up** (page 103-104). The only difference is in *removing manipulatives* instead of adding them. For example, in the subtraction problem 16.34 - 9.26, Partner A builds 16.34 and Partner B takes away 9.26, regrouping if needed.

ACTIVITY 7.4

Mix-Freeze-Add (or Subtract)

Cooperative Structure:
Mix-Freeze-Pair

Make copies of the **Decimal Number Cards** (pages 159-162). Cut them apart and give each student one. Follow the basic steps of Mix-Freeze-Pair, asking students to bring paper and pencil with them as they mix. After they freeze and pair, have them show each other their **Decimal Number Cards** and add (or subtract) them according to your directions. Each person computes the answer individually first, then the two compare solutions. Continue with additional rounds of Mix-Freeze-Pair, having students swap cards with their partner after each round.

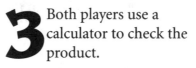

Buzzing for Products

Students take turns selecting factors to multiply. They score points based on the value of the product in relation to several target numbers.

Steps...

1 Give each pair one **Buzzing for Products** (page 111) game board, one calculator, and a handful of game markers.

2 The first player selects two numbers by placing markers on two different bees.

3 Both players use a calculator to check the product.

4 The person selecting the numbers scores the appropriate points according to which hive the product falls into.

5 Players take turns selecting numbers to multiply. Players may only select numbers which are not already covered.

6 Points are tallied at the end of the game.

7 Players praise each other and discuss winning strategies.

8 Game boards are cleared and players switch partners.

Variations...

- **Combined Points**- Instead of competing against each other, have students keep a running tally of their combined points. Let them play several times and try to beat their best score.

- **Create a Learning Center**- Buzzing for Products works well in a learning center. You can use it as a part of a Rotation Learning Center review or set it up as a Learning Choice Center. Refer to pages 14-15 for more information about centers.

Cooperative Structure

Play-N-Switch

Materials

- **Buzzing for Products** game boards (1 per pair)
- Game markers in two colors (bingo chips, pattern blocks, dried beans, etc.)
- Calculators (1 per person)

Getting Ready

Review estimation of decimals. In addition review concepts of comparing and ordering decimals. You may want to demonstrate the scoring method in advance using a few practice problems.

Buzzing For Products

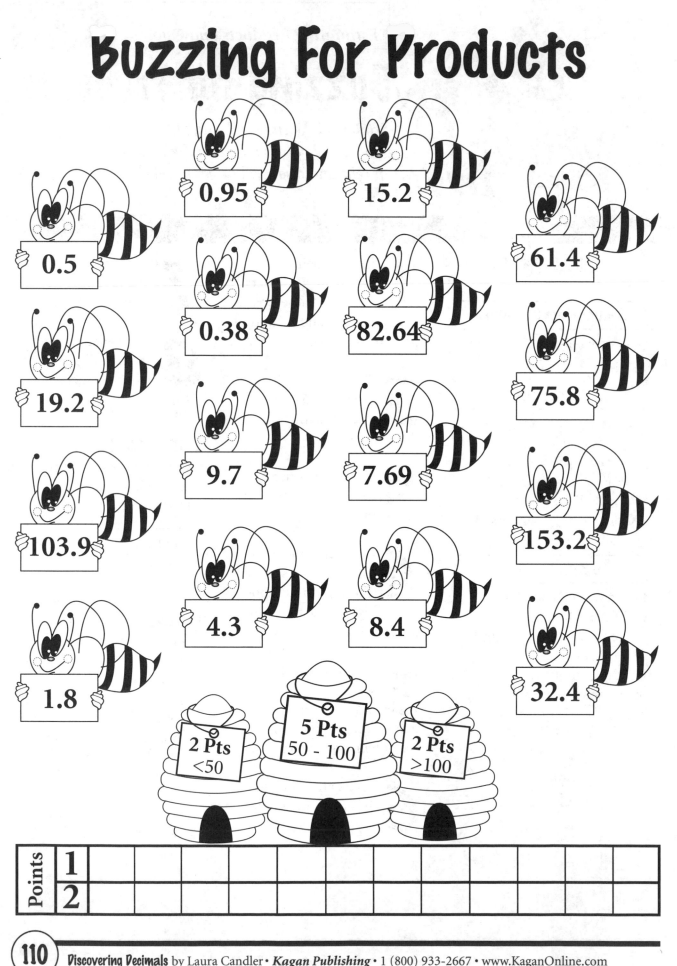

Discovering Decimals by Laura Candler • *Kagan Publishing* • 1 (800) 933-2667 • www.KaganOnline.com

ACTIVITY 8.2

Estimation Check

Cooperative Structure:
Pairs Check

Write multiplication and/or division computation problems in the boxes of a blank **Pairs Check Form** worksheet (page 165). Instead of having students find the exact answers, have them estimate the solutions and explain their estimation methods to their partner and team.

ACTIVITY 8.3

Estimation Match

Cooperative Structure:
Mix-N-Match

Prepare the problem and answer cards in advance or have the students use the blank **Mix-N-Match Patterns** (page 166) to prepare the cards before the activity. Write one decimal problem (multiplication and/or division) on each square. Write each problem's estimated answer on the corresponding octagon. Cut apart the cards and follow the basic **Mix-N-Match** directions.

ACTIVITY 8.4

Estimate Around

Cooperative Structure:
RoundRobin

Use index cards to prepare a set of estimation problems. Stack the problems face down in the center of the team. Have each student, in turn, flip over the top card, read the problem aloud, and estimate the answer using mental math. Encourage students to talk through the steps they use. For example, "First I round 12.81 to 13. Then I round 2.13 to 2. Finally I multiply 13 and 2 to get 26."

Additional Activities

Moving Ahead with Multiplication

Students use Base 10 manipulatives to model simple decimal multiplication problems. After each problem, students travel to a new team to share and discuss the answer.

$$
\begin{array}{r}
2.58 \\
\times\ 3 \\
\hline
7.74
\end{array}
$$

S t e p s . . .

Cooperative Structure

**RoundTable,
Traveling Heads (Numbered Heads** Variation)

Materials

- **Base 10 Manipulatives**
  (1 set per team)
- **Place Value Mats**
  (1 per team)
- **Moving Ahead with Multiplication** transparency
- Paper and pencil

Getting Ready

Make sure you have enough **Base 10 Manipulatives** (pages 155-156) for each team to have one set. Each set should have at least 2 cubes, 20 flats, 30 rods, and 50 units. Prepare a **Place Value Mat** for each team following the directions on page 154. Make a transparency of the **Moving Ahead With Multiplication** page.

1 Number students off from 1 to 4. Put a **Place Value Mat** and a set of **Base 10 Manipulatives** in the center of each team. Place the transparency on the overhead.

2 Write a simple multiplication problem such as 2.58 X 3 on the board. Use the suggested list or make up your own involving a decimal times a whole number. (See **Moving Ahead With Multiplication** at right.)

3 Refer to the transparency as you explain the procedure. Ask Person #1 to build the number 2.58 on his or her desk. Since the number will be multiplied by 3, ask Persons #2 and #3 to build the number also.

4 Have all 3 students place their manipulatives (2 flats, 5 rods, and 8 units each) on the **Place Value Mat** in the appropriate locations.

Moving Ahead With Multiplication

5.17 x 3
6.8 x 2
2.45 x 4
4.8 x 3
1.34 x 5
2.09 x 4
3.72 x 2

5 Ask Person #4 to count up the number in each column, starting with the units first. If there are more than 10, they regroup using rods. Then they count the total number of rods and regroup, if needed, using flats. Finally, the flats are counted and regrouped.

6 Together, the team discusses the final product and everyone writes down the answer.

7 Randomly choose a number from 1 to 4. The person on each

Moving Ahead With Multiplication

2.58
x 3
7.74

team with that number moves ahead to the next team and checks that team's answer and Base 10 arrangement.

8 Call on one person to share the answer with the class.

9 Present a new problem. Make sure students continue to take turns in RoundTable fashion as they handle the manipulatives.

Hints...

- **Modeling** - When you introduce this skill, you may want to have the class gather around one team as you guide this group to model the steps for the class.

- **Choosing Random Numbers** - Use a Numbered Heads spinner or a Student Selector to choose a number (both are available from *Kagan Publishing*). If you don't have a spinner, roll a regular 6-sided die. If a 5 or 6 comes up, call it "teacher choice" and select a number that hasn't responded so far.

- **Rotation Patterns** - During each round, change the number of teams the "traveling" student moves. In this way the activity serves as a classbuilder, since brand new teams will form after four or five rounds.

- **Linking Concrete and Abstract Concepts** - After having students solve several multiplication problems using **Base 10 Manipulatives**, start writing each problem on the board. Solve the problem step-by-step on the board as students solve it with their manipulatives. Later in the lesson, have them solve problems by drawing Base 10 block illustrations. Finally, teach them to multiply without manipulatives or pictures.

Moving Ahead With Multiplication

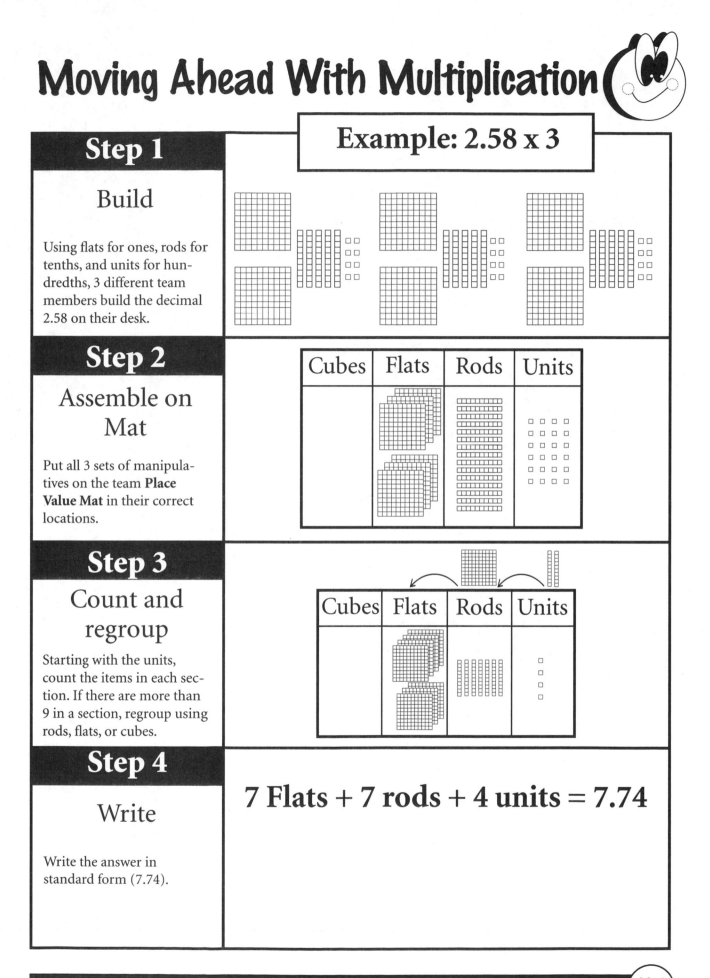

Step 1	**Example: 2.58 x 3**
Build Using flats for ones, rods for tenths, and units for hundredths, 3 different team members build the decimal 2.58 on their desk.	

Step 2

Assemble on Mat

Put all 3 sets of manipulatives on the team **Place Value Mat** in their correct locations.

Cubes	Flats	Rods	Units

Step 3

Count and regroup

Starting with the units, count the items in each section. If there are more than 9 in a section, regroup using rods, flats, or cubes.

Cubes	Flats	Rods	Units

Step 4

Write

Write the answer in standard form (7.74).

7 Flats + 7 rods + 4 units = 7.74

Purple Products

To solve simple multiplication problems, partners color a decimal grid using red and blue crayons. The product (where the two colors intersect) will appear in purple. Pairs Compare their answers to check for correctness.

$$\begin{array}{r} 0.2 \\ \times\ 0.3 \\ \hline 0.06 \end{array}$$

Cooperative Structure

Pairs Compare

Materials

- 1 Copy of **Purple Products** for each pair
- 1 Red and 1 blue crayon or colored pencil for each pair

Getting Ready

Make an overhead transparency of the **Decimal Squares** (page 158). Prepare students for this multiplication activity by demonstrating how to color a grid to find the product of two decimals. Using one block of the transparent 100 square grid on the overhead projector, color one factor (such as 0.3) *horizontally* in red. Color the other factor (such as 0.4) *vertically* in blue. The purple area where the two colors cross is the product (in this case 0.12).

Steps...

1 Divide teams into 2 sets of pairs. Designate Partners A and B.

2 Partner A colors the first factor *horizontally in red*.

3 Partner B colors the second factor *vertically in blue*.

4 Together the students count the purple squares to find the product. One person writes the product on the line below the problem.

5 Students continue to work all 8 problems, taking turns to record their answers.

6 When everyone is finished, the entire team compares and discusses answers.

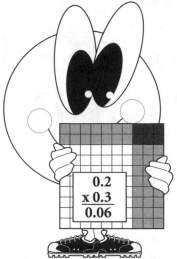

Purple Products

Partner A colors the first decimal horizontally in red. Partner B colors the second decimal vertically in blue. The area in purple shows the product of the two decimals. Compare answers with your teammates after everyone has finished all 8 problems.

Partner A _____

Partner B _____

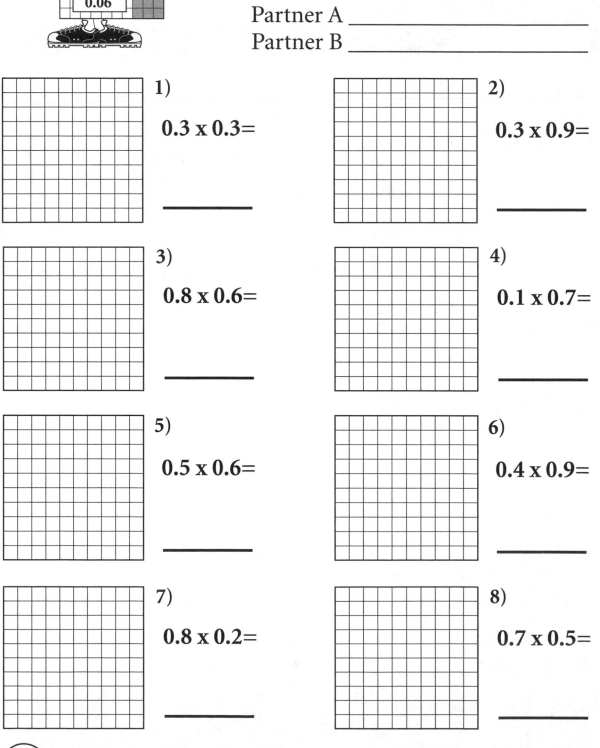

1)

0.3 x 0.3 =

_____

2)

0.3 x 0.9 =

_____

3)

0.8 x 0.6 =

_____

4)

0.1 x 0.7 =

_____

5)

0.5 x 0.6 =

_____

6)

0.4 x 0.9 =

_____

7)

0.8 x 0.2 =

_____

8)

0.7 x 0.5 =

_____

Discovering Decimals by Laura Candler • **Kagan Publishing** • 1 (800) 933-2667 • www.KaganOnline.com

$$\begin{array}{r} 2.73 \\ 3{\overline{\smash{)}\,8.19}} \end{array}$$

Break It Down

Students use Base 10 manipulatives to solve simple decimal division problems. After each problem is solved, the problem card is rotated to the next team.

Steps . . .

Cooperative Structure

RoundTable
Send-A-Problem

Materials

- **Base 10 Manipulatives** (1 set per team)
- **Place Value Mat** (1 per team)
- **Break It Down Division Problems** (1 per class)
- **Break It Down Example** transparency
- Paper and pencil
- Calculators (1 per team only)

Getting Ready

This activity works best if students have already done "**Moving Ahead With Multiplication**" (pages 113-115). The steps are very similar except that students are passing the problems ahead to the next team rather than moving ahead with their answer. You'll need a set of **Base 10 Manipulatives** (pages 155-156) for each team, with at least 1 cube, 10 flats, 10 rods, and 10 units in each set. If you don't have **Place Value Mats**, you can prepare them using the directions (page 154). Make a transparency of the **Break It Down Example** (page 121).

1 Place the **Base 10 Manipulatives** and **Place Value Mat** in the center of each team. Place the **Break It Down** transparency on the overhead projector.

2 Use one team to model the directions for Base 10 block division. As the rest of the class watches, have the students take turns following the steps on the overhead transparency. The first person does Step 1, the next does Step 2, and so on in RoundTable fashion. The last person records the team answer and checks it with a calculator.

3 After everyone understands the procedure, give each team one **Break It Down Problem Card** (page 122). The team follows the steps on the overhead to find the quotient.

4 When all teams are ready, have one person pass the **Break It Down Problem Card** to the next team.

5 As students begin a new problem, they rotate roles one person to the left. A different person builds the dividend for each round.

Hints...

- **Extra Problem Cards** - You may want to prepare a few extra **Break It Down Problem Cards**. That way if a team always finishes early you can give them an extra problem to work on while they are waiting.

- **Paper and Pencil Division** - If some teams finish before others are ready, ask them to write the division problem on paper and try to work it out "the long way." They will be amazed that they get the same answer as they did with **Base 10 Manipulatives**.

- **Linking Concrete and Abstract Concepts** - After having students solve several division problems using **Base 10 Manipula-**

Break It Down

$$\begin{array}{r} 2.73 \\ 3\overline{)\,8.19} \end{array}$$

tives, start writing each problem on the board. Solve the problem step-by-step on the board as students solve it with their manipulatives. Later in the lesson, have them solve problems by drawing Base 10 block illustrations. Finally, teach them to divide without manipulatives or pictures.

Break It Down

Example: $3\overline{)8.19}$

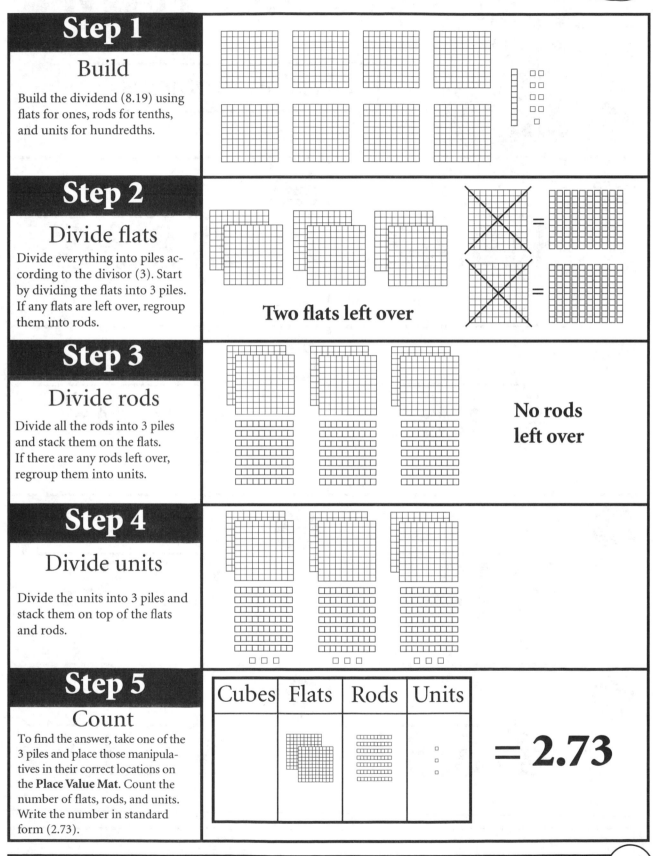

Step 1

Build

Build the dividend (8.19) using flats for ones, rods for tenths, and units for hundredths.

Step 2

Divide flats

Divide everything into piles according to the divisor (3). Start by dividing the flats into 3 piles. If any flats are left over, regroup them into rods.

Two flats left over

Step 3

Divide rods

Divide all the rods into 3 piles and stack them on the flats. If there are any rods left over, regroup them into units.

No rods left over

Step 4

Divide units

Divide the units into 3 piles and stack them on top of the flats and rods.

Step 5

Count

To find the answer, take one of the 3 piles and place those manipulatives in their correct locations on the **Place Value Mat**. Count the number of flats, rods, and units. Write the number in standard form (2.73).

Cubes	Flats	Rods	Units

$= 2.73$

Break It Down

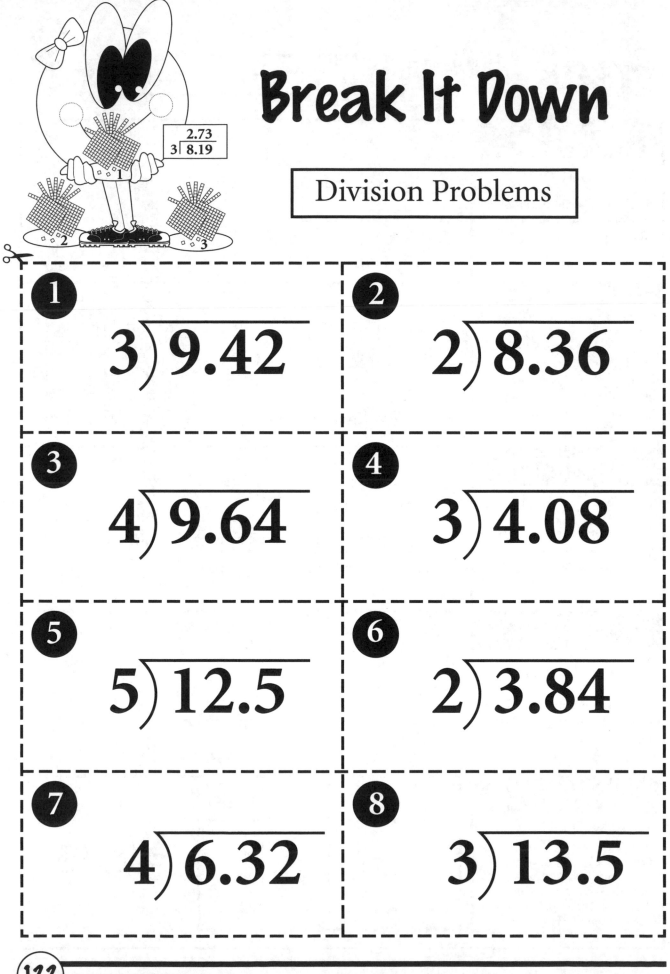

$$3 \overline{)\, 2.73 \atop 8.19}$$

Division Problems

1 $3 \overline{)\, 9.42}$

2 $2 \overline{)\, 8.36}$

3 $4 \overline{)\, 9.64}$

4 $3 \overline{)\, 4.08}$

5 $5 \overline{)\, 12.5}$

6 $2 \overline{)\, 3.84}$

7 $4 \overline{)\, 6.32}$

8 $3 \overline{)\, 13.5}$

Discovering Decimals by Laura Candler • *Kagan Publishing* • 1 (800) 933-2667 • www.KaganOnline.com

ACTIVITY 9.4

Pairs Check Practice

Cooperative Structure:
Pairs Check

Write multiplication and/or division problems on a blank **Pairs Check Form** (page 165). Follow the basic Pairs Check directions, allowing students to use a calculator during the final stage to check the accuracy of answers.

ACTIVITY 9.5

Buzzing for Products

Cooperative Structure:
Play-N-Switch

Have students play **Buzzing for Products** (page 109) using only 1 calculator per pair. One person works the problem out with paper and pencil while the other uses the calculator to check the product. Students switch roles throughout the game.

ACTIVITY 9.6

Computation Showdown

Cooperative Structure:
Showdown

Use index cards or the blank **Showdown Task Card** (page 164) form to prepare a set of cards containing multiplication and division problems. Place the cards face down in the center of each team, and have students proceed according to the basic Showdown directions. Allow the Turn Captain to use a calculator to check the team's answer for each round.

ACTIVITY 9.7

Discovering Patterns

Cooperative Structure:
Think-Pair-Share

Think-Pair-Share is great to use when teaching students about multiplication and division patterns with multiples of 10. For example, you can show a multiplication pattern such as "3.21 x 10 = 32.1, 3.21 x 100 = 321 and 3.21 x 1000 = 3,210." Then have them Think-Pair-Share their responses to this question: "What pattern did you notice in these problems?" Next, put up a new pattern and leave off the last answer. Ask students to Think-Write-Pair-Share the number that would go in the blank.

Additional Activities

0.4

Team Answer $\frac{4}{10}$

Decimals Into Fractions

Team members individually convert decimals into fractions, then compare and discuss answers with teammates.

Steps . . .

1 Students cut apart **Decimals Into Fractions Task Cards** (page 126) and place them face down in center of team.

2 Students number off 1-4. Person #1 becomes first Turn Captain.

3 Turn Captain flips over the first problem card.

4 Everyone works the problem individually by writing the decimal in fraction form on their response board.

5 Turn Captain says, "Showdown!" Team members show answers, then compare and discuss solutions.

6 Turn Captain records the team answer on the problem card and places it in a separate pile.

7 Circulate and check team answers. Offer hints and help as needed.

Cooperative Structure

Showdown

Materials

- **Decimals Into Fractions Task Cards** for each team
- Scissors
- Individual chalkboards or other response boards

Getting Ready

This activity works well for review and practice. Demonstrate how to change a decimal into a fraction by using a multiple of 10 in the denominator. Tell students whether or not you expect answers to be reduced to lowest terms.

Decimals Into Fractions Task Cards

0.4
Team Answer $\frac{4}{10}$

0.5
Team Answer_____

0.25
Team Answer_____

0.6
Team Answer_____

0.20
Team Answer_____

0.75
Team Answer_____

0.8
Team Answer_____

0.35
Team Answer_____

0.05
Team Answer_____

0.68
Team Answer_____

0.16
Team Answer_____

 Discovering Decimals by Laura Candler • *Kagan Publishing* • 1 (800) 933-2667 • www.KaganOnline.com

ACTIVITY
10.2

Decimal Percent Match

Cooperative Structure:
Mix-N-Match

Using one **Mix-N-Match Pattern** worksheet (page 166) per team, write decimals in the squares and the corresponding percents in the octagons. Be sure to include challenging number pairs such as 0.03 - 3% and 0.3 - 30%. Distribute one card to each student and follow the basic Mix-N-Match directions.

ACTIVITY
10.3

Decimal Fraction Match

Cooperative Structure:
Mix-N-Match

Prepare the Mix-N-Match cards by following the directions for the Decimal Percent Match to the left, but substitute fractions for percents. Give one card to each student and follow the basic structure directions. If appropriate, let students carry calculators with them to assist in converting fractions to decimals.

ACTIVITY
10.4

Percents Into Decimals

Cooperative Structure:
Think-Pair-Share

Write 0.75 on the board and demonstrate how to change a decimal into a percent. Then write a new decimal on the board and ask students to mentally convert it into a percent. Have students think about their answer and then pair with a partner to discuss their answers. Call on one person to share the answer with the class. Repeat with new numbers.

Additional Activities

Pet Shop Problem Solving

Students solve multi-step word problems by discussing strategies and writing individual responses.

S t e p s . . .

Cooperative Structure

Teammates Consult

Materials

- Calculators (1 per student)
- **Pet Shop Problem Solving** worksheet (1 per student)
- Poster or transparency of **Mathematicians Consult Student Directions**
- Large cup for pencils (1 per team - optional)

Getting Ready

Duplicate one copy of the **Pet Shop Problem Solving** (page 130) worksheet for each student. Make a transparency or poster of the **Mathematicians Consult Student Directions** (page 44). Review proper methods for using a calculator to solve decimal problems. Remind students that a calculator drops ending zeros which appear to the left of the decimal point.

1 Distribute materials and place the **Mathematicians Consult Student Directions** on the overhead. Place the cup in the center of the team to hold pencils.

2 Refer to the overhead transparency as you explain the directions step-by-step. Choose a team to model the steps for the class as you read the directions.

3 Leave the directions up as the teams work through the **Pet Shop Problem Solving** activity.

4 Monitor the teams carefully, and remind students that talking is only allowed *when their pencils are in the cup*. Students are not permitted to ask for help when they are writing their answers.

Hints...

- **Time Limits** -If kitchen timers or egg timers are available, you may want to limit the time allowed for team discussion. Sometimes students who don't agree on the solution waste valuable team time. Remind them that everyone does not have to agree on the answer; after a suitable period of discussion they should "agree to disagree" and write their own responses.

Pet Shop
Problem Solving

Name_____

---

1. Sonya and Donald work at Pet Paradise during the summer. One of Sonya's jobs is to keep the aquarium filled. The aquarium contains 18.7 gallons of water. If she adds 2.9 gallons, how many gallons will be in the aquarium in all?

Answer: _____
Explanation: _____
_____
_____
_____
_____
_____

---

2. Donald feeds the dogs each morning. This morning, the store owner gave him two bags of dog food—a full 5 pound bag and one weighing only 3.4 pounds. Donald was told to give each of the 14 dogs exactly the same amount of dog food. How much did he measure out for each dog?

Answer: _____
Explanation: _____
_____
_____
_____
_____
_____

---

3. Pet Paradise sells bird seed for $1.20 a pound. Sonya poured three large scoops into a bag for a customer and found that it weighed 2.7 pounds. The same customer also bought a bird cage for $15.95. How much did the customer owe in all?

Answer: _____
Explanation: _____
_____
_____
_____
_____
_____

---

4. Donald weighed each of Pet Paradise's four kittens. The first weighed 2.79 lbs, the second was exactly 3 lbs, the third was 2.65 lbs, and the last one weighed only 2.2 pounds. What was the average weight of a kitten at Pet Paradise?

Answer: _____
Explanation: _____
_____
_____
_____
_____
_____

 Discovering Decimals by Laura Candler • *Kagan Publishing* • 1 (800) 933-2667 • www.KaganOnline.com

Better Buy Bargains

Each team is given a different "better buy" problem to solve. After the answers are recorded, problems are rotated to new teams.

Steps . . .

1 Give each team a different problem card and one answer page.

2 Number students off from 1 to 4. Person #1 on each team becomes the first Leader.

3 Ask the Leader to read the problem aloud.

4 Everyone discusses the problem and works it on their calculator.

5 The Leader checks individual answers and guides the team to agree on the correct solution. Everyone discusses how to word the explanation.

6 The Leader records the team answer and explanation in the correct block on the answer page.

7 When all the teams are ready, the Leader (Person #1) delivers the problem to the new Leader (Person #2) on the next team.

8 Continue as time allows, rotating Leaders each round.

Hints...

- **Unit Prices** - Remind Leaders to include the unit price of each item in their explanations.

- **Time Limits** - If some teams are much slower than others, set a time limit for each round (perhaps 5 or 10 minutes). Give a reminder 2 minutes before the time is up, and expect teams to pass the problems when the final time limit is announced.

- **Leader Responsibilities** - Review the responsibilities of the Leader and post a list on the board such as the one on the following page.

Cooperative Structure

Send-A-Problem

Materials

- Set of 8 **Better Buy Bargains** problem cards (1 set per class)
- **Better Buy Bargains** answer pages (1 per team)
- Calculators (1 per person if possible, 1 per team minimum)
- Scrap paper and pencil

Getting Ready

Introduce the "better buy" concept to the class using real objects if possible. For example, show them a 6 oz. can of tomato sauce costing $0.48 and a 15 oz. can costing $0.90. Ask, "Which one is the better buy?" Allow time for team discussion, then discuss solutions as a class. Explain that one way to solve these problems involves finding the unit cost of the items, which is the cost per ounce in this example.

Make one copy of the **Better Buy Bargains** (page 134) worksheet for the class and cut the 8 **Better Buy Bargain** problem cards apart. You may want to laminate them prior to use.

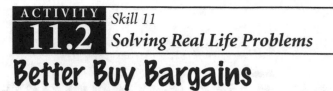

Leader Responsibilities

- Read the problem aloud clearly.
- Keep everyone on task.
- Check individual answers and lead discussion.
- Write the team answer on the worksheet.
- Take the problem to the next team.

Better Buy Bargains

Problems

1 Rebecca wants to buy cupcakes. She can buy 2 for $0.48 or 5 cupcakes for $1.25. Which is the better buy? Explain your answer.

2 Thomas is shopping for chicken. One brand has a 3 lb. package for $5.25. Another brand has a 2 lb. package for $3.60. Which package is the better buy? Explain your answer.

3 A 2 liter bottle of Cola sells for $1.28 and a 3 liter bottle is $2.04. Which bottle is the better buy? Explain your answer.

4 Judy found a 6 oz. can of orange juice for $0.72 and a 9 oz. can for $1.17. Which is the better buy and why?

5 Which is the better buy: a 5 oz. container of yogurt for $0.75 or an 8 oz. carton for $1.12? Explain your answer.

6 Tonya wants to buy toothpaste. She can choose between a 6 oz. tube for $1.26 or an 8 oz. tube for $1.60. Which is the better buy and why?

7 Sweetsie Donuts are sold in 2 package sizes. One box contains 6 donuts for $0.72. The other box has a dozen for $1.92. Which is the better buy? Explain your answer.

8 Terry needs 8 oz. of tomato paste for her spaghetti sauce. Should she buy several 4 oz. cans costing $0.60 each or the 10 oz. can for $1.00? Explain your answer.

Better Buy Bargains

Team Answers

1 Answer: _____
Reason: _____
_____
_____
_____

2 Answer: _____
Reason: _____
_____
_____
_____

3 Answer: _____
Reason: _____
_____
_____
_____

4 Answer: _____
Reason: _____
_____
_____
_____

5 Answer: _____
Reason: _____
_____
_____
_____

6 Answer: _____
Reason: _____
_____
_____
_____

7 Answer: _____
Reason: _____
_____
_____
_____

8 Answer: _____
Reason: _____
_____
_____
_____

Discovering Decimals by Laura Candler • *Kagan Publishing* • 1 (800) 933-2667 • www.KaganOnline.com

Send-A-Menu

Each team creates its own restaurant menu and set of menu-based word problems. Menus and problems are rotated from team to team for problem-solving practice.

Cooperative Structure

RoundTable
Send-A-Problem

Materials

- **Today's Menu** handout (1 per team)
- Calculators (1 per person or at least 1 per team)
- Crayons, colored pencils, or markers
- Index cards or 6" x 9" slips of paper (1 per person)

Getting Ready

If possible, bring in a few examples of restaurant menus (many restaurants have paper copies they are willing to share). Discuss menu terms like appetizer, beverage, and special.

Note: this lesson takes at least 2 days to complete.

Steps...

1 Ask each team to invent a restaurant and make up a name for their eating establishment. While they are discussing their ideas and choosing a name, distribute copies of the **Today's Menu** handout (page 137) and other materials.

2 Have one person use a crayon or marker to write the restaurant name at the top of the menu.

3 Each person is responsible for completing one section of the menu in RoundTable fashion. As the menu is passed from person to person, the entire team discusses ideas for food items. Each team member writes the names and prices of three different items in their section. Teams may color or decorate their menus if time permits.

4 When the menu is complete, each person makes up a word problem using the information on the team menu. He or she writes the problem on one side of an index card and the answer on the back.

5 Team members swap index cards and use calculators to check for clarity and accuracy.

6 Follow the basic Send-A-Problem directions, making sure teams send both the menu and the set of word problem cards. Instead of writing down the team answers, the team Leader for each round turns over the index card to see if his or her team has found the correct answer. If the answers don't match, the team continues to work on the problem.

Hints...

- **Teacher Checks Problems** - You may want to collect the word problems cards and check them for accuracy *before* starting the Send-A-Problem part of this activity. Doing so will eliminate confusion due to poorly worded problems and incorrect solutions.

Send-A-Menu

- **Creative Menus** - Instead of using the **Today's Menu** worksheet, give teams construction paper, scissors, and glue to create their own unique menus. This will take longer, but the process is a true teambuilding activity and is well-worth the time spent.

- **Calculator Use** - Be sure to let students use calculators when solving word problems. This allows them to focus on strategies rather than computation.

Today's Menu

Regular Items | Price

_____ | _____

_____ | _____

Specials

_____ | _____

_____ | _____

_____ | _____

Beverages

_____ | _____

_____ | _____

Desserts

_____ | _____

_____ | _____

_____ | _____

Movie Madness

Students in teams solve word problems by interpreting a chart of movie theater prices. A number is announced and one team member travels to the next team to share the answer.

S t e p s . . .

1 Number students off 1 to 4. Place a copy of the **Movie Madness Theater Prices** chart in the center of each team and give one calculator to each person.

2 Place Problem #1 on the overhead. Have each person try to figure out the answer using a calculator to check work.

3 Ask all students to compare and discuss answers. The team needs to agree on one correct solution only.

4 Spin the spinner or roll the die to randomly choose a number. (If a 5 or 6 comes up, it's "teacher choice.")

5 Students with that number stand and "travel" to a new team. They share their team's answer along with the steps of the solution. Team members praise or help the newcomers as needed.

6 Call on one student to explain the correct answer to the entire class.

7 Place Problem #2 on the overhead. Follow the same steps as above, but don't allow students to travel to teams already having a member of their original team. Continue with the remaining problems.

Hints...

- **Assign Team Rotation** - If you don't want numbered students to choose where they will "travel", assign the team rotation. For example, say "Person #1, travel 1 team over." For the next round, have Person #2, move 2 teams and so on. In this manner, no one will end up with an old teammate.

- **Monitor Carefully** - Move about the room as students work and make sure everyone is attempting to solve each problem individually before discussing it with the team.

Cooperative Structure

Traveling Heads
(**Numbered Heads** Variation)

Materials

- **Movie Madness** chart (1 per team)
- **Movie Madness Word Problems** transparency (1 per class)
- Paper and pencil
- Calculators (1 per person if possible)
- Numbered Heads spinner or 6-sided die

Getting Ready

Duplicate one copy of the **Move Madness Theater Prices** (page 140) chart for each team. Make a transparency of the word problems (or duplicate one copy per team).

Movie Madness

Movie Theater Prices

Theater	Child	Adult	Senior Citizen
Max's Movie House	$4.25	$4.25	$4.25
Bargain Cinema	$3.50	$4.75	$4.50
All Star Cinema	$4.25	$6.00	$4.00
Bayview Theater	$5.00	$7.25	$5.00
Royal Cinema	$4.50	$6.75	$4.50

 Discovering Decimals by Laura Candler • Kagan Publishing • 1 (800) 933-2667 • www.KaganOnline.com

Movie Madness

Problem 1

Jessica and her three friends went to see *Star Voyage* at Max's Movie House. How much did they pay in all for their tickets?

Problem 2

Tamara's grandfather, a senior citizen, took her and her brother to the All Star Cinema. Tamara and her brother got children's tickets. How much did her grandfather pay in all?

Problem 3

Mr. Thomas bought 2 children's tickets and 2 adult tickets at the Bargain Cinema. He paid with a $20 bill. How much change did he get back?

Problem 4

Mrs. Avis took her 2 children to the movies and paid exactly $17.25 for the 3 tickets. Which movie theater did she take them to?

Problem 5

Mrs. Davis invited four friends to the movies. Three of the ladies were senior citizens. Which theater would be the least expensive? How much would she pay in all?

ACTIVITY 11.5

Taxing Problems

Cooperative Structure:
Numbered Heads Together

Number students off from 1 to 4. Give each team an advertising flyer from the same store. Demonstrate how to figure sales tax on an item. Name a particular item in the flyer. Have students find the item and figure the sales tax individually. (Depending on your objective, let students work problems on a calculator or with paper and pencil only.) Then have them compare and discuss answers. Randomly choose a number and have those students write the answer on a response board to show the class. Be sure to call on at least one person to explain how their team arrived at the answer. Repeat with new items, making sure you call on different students to respond.

ACTIVITY 11.6

Team Problem Solving Practice

Cooperative Structure:
Showdown

This structure is excellent for having students solve word problems. Use the blank **Showdown Task Cards** (page 164) blackline to prepare a set of decimal word problem cards, or find an appropriate set of problems in your math text. Have students follow the basic Showdown directions, but be sure to have the Turn Captain record the team answer on the task card. Circulate among teams to check and discuss solutions.

ACTIVITY 11.7

Paired Problem Solving

Cooperative Structure:
Pairs Compare

Using a textbook or teacher-prepared set of word problems, ask students to work in pairs to discuss and solve the problems. Be sure each pair has only one calculator and one sheet to record answers. Have them take turns using the calculator and recording answers. When they have finished with all problems, ask them to Pairs Compare with another pair of students who are also finished.

Additional Activities

ACTIVITY 11.8
Textbook Word Problems

Cooperative Structure:
Teammates Consult

Teammates Consult works well with any set of challenging word problems. After students become familiar with the format, have them use this structure any time they complete word problems, even those in the textbook. Just place the **"Mathematicians Consult"** (page 44) transparency on the overhead. Then have students write their answers (including a written explanation of the solution) on a regular sheet of notebook paper.

Additional Activities

ACTIVITY 11.9
Traveling Solutions

Cooperative Structure:
Traveling Heads (**Numbered Heads** Variation)

Use word problems found in your textbook or on a worksheet. Each team needs one copy or one book. Number students off from 1 to 4. Everyone solves the first problem using a calculator, then team members check and discuss answers. When all teams are ready, call a number. The person with that number on each team "travels" to the next team and shares the team answer. The students listen to the new team member's solution and offer praise or help as needed. Repeat with each problem. Call a different number each time, and announce a different number of teams for the traveler to move. For example, "Person #2 move 3 teams over." This way the teams will be randomly mixed after several rounds.

Decimal Bingo

BINGO!

Students in teams use decimal skills to play bingo cooperatively.

S t e p s . . .

1 Write the answers to the **Decimal Bingo** problems on the board.

2 Give each team one **Decimal Bingo** board. In RoundTable fashion, have them pass the game board around the team and randomly write 16 of the answers in the blocks.

3 Place a pile of game markers on one side of the board and a set of **Decimal Bingo Problem Cards** *face up* on the other side.

4 All team members work the top problem individually.

5 When everyone is ready, Person #1 leads the team in comparing and discussing answers. The team must agree on *one correct answer.*

6 Person #1 turns over the top card to check the answer. If the team

answer was correct, Person #1 may cover the number with a marker. If not, the team moves to the next problem without placing a marker.

7 Person #2 becomes the leader for the next round. Leaders rotate each round, and the game continues until one row of answers is covered (horizontally, vertically, or diagonally).

Variations...

- **Send-A-Problem** - Prepare a different set of problem cards for each team. When all team are finished with the first bingo game, have them rotate the problem cards to another team.

Hints...

- **Monitor Carefully** - Make sure all students are attempting to work the problems individually before comparing answers. If someone has a different answer, make sure the team discusses the solution rather than using a "majority rules" approach.

Cooperative Structure

**RoundTable
Showdown**

Materials

- **Decimal Bingo** game boards (1 per team)
- **Decimal Bingo Problem Cards** (see "Getting Ready" above)
- Answers (see page 171)
- Game markers (16 per team)
- Scrap paper or response boards

Getting Ready

Duplicate one **Decimal Bingo** game board (page 147) per person. Duplicate and cut apart all 20 of the **Decimal Bingo Problem Cards** (page 148-149) provided or make your own set. An easy way to create your own is to make up 16 or more review problems and write them in the blocks on two blank **Showdown Task Cards** (page 164) forms. Duplicate one set for each team, cut them apart, and write the answers on the backs of the cards.

Decimal Bingo

- **Learning Center Use - Decimal Bingo** works very well in any type of learning center. Prepare the game boards and problem cards in advance and laminate them for future use. You can even prepare a variety of different problem cards so that students can play the game repeatedly and practice many skills.

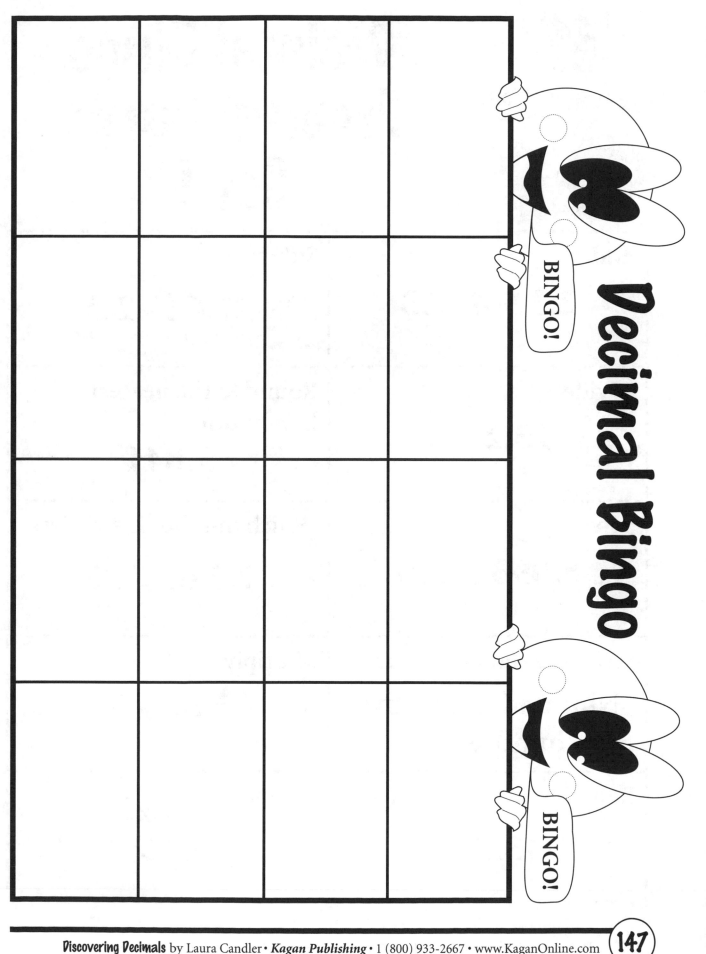

Decimal Bingo

BINGO!

BINGO!

Decimal Bingo Problem Cards Set 1

Add	Subtract
2.3 + 48.68	**27.64 - 2.3**

Divide	Round to the nearest hundredth
15.2 ÷ 4	**9.841**

Solve	Which number is smaller?
5.098 x 100	**7.1 or 7.35**

Write the standard form	Multiply
Nine and eighty-five hundredths	**5.68 x 7**

Round to the nearest tenth	Estimate
3.85	**9.23** **+4.9**

Decimal Bingo Problem Cards Set 2

BINGO!

Estimate **43.98 - 17.64**	Add **4.2 + 65.95 + 103.4**
Round to the nearest whole number **13.261**	Subtract **55 - 23.5**

Add   **40.3**
         56.94
         0.78
     +25.6
	Estimate
	
	19.6 x 3

Multiply **34.77** **x 5**	Divide **36.75 ÷ 5**
Estimate **79.7 ÷ 8**	Which number is larger? **123.62 or 123.7**

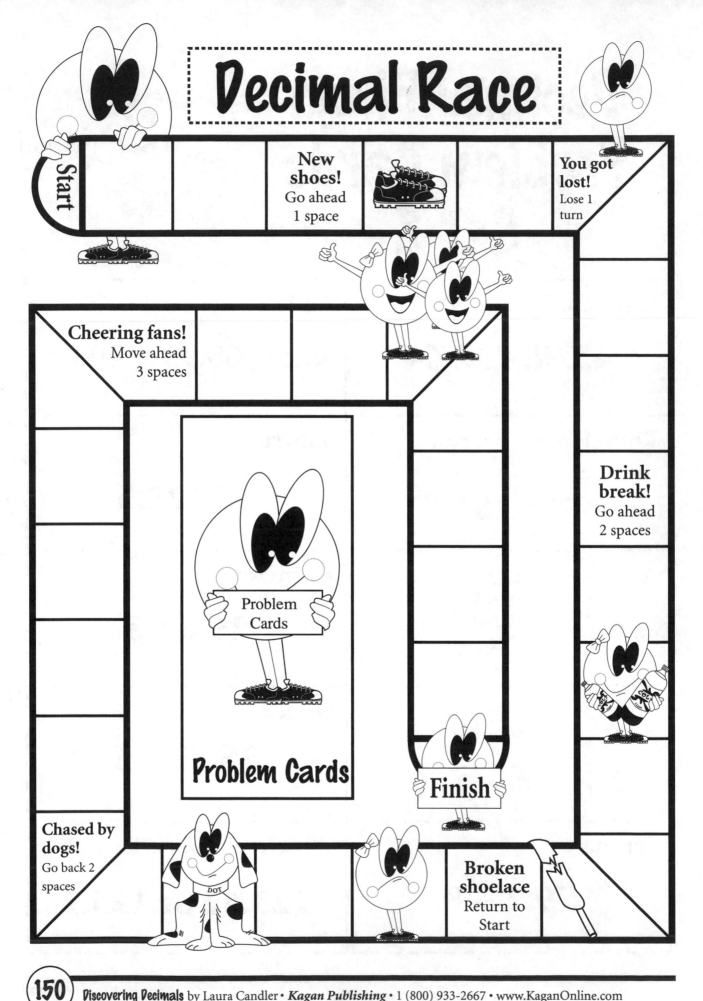

Decimal Race

Start

New shoes!
Go ahead
1 space

You got lost!
Lose 1 turn

Cheering fans!
Move ahead
3 spaces

Drink break!
Go ahead
2 spaces

Problem Cards

Problem Cards

Finish

Chased by dogs!
Go back 2 spaces

Broken shoelace
Return to Start

Discovering Decimals by Laura Candler • *Kagan Publishing* • 1 (800) 933-2667 • www.KaganOnline.com

ACTIVITY 12.2

Decimal Race

Cooperative Structure:
Play-N-Switch

Use the **Decimal Race** game board (page 150). Prepare a set of **Decimal Bingo Problem Cards** (pages 148-149) by cutting index cards in half. Write one decimal problem on the front of each card and its answer on the back. Pair students and give each pair one game board, two game markers, and one die. Players place the problem cards face up in the middle of the board. They both work the top problem, then turn over the problem card to check its answer. The player or players with the correct answer individually roll the die to determine how many spaces to move forward.

This activity works very well in any type of learning center. Prepare the game boards and problem cards in advance and laminate them for future use. You can even prepare a variety of different problem cards so that students can play the game repeatedly and practice many skills.

ACTIVITY 12.3

Partner Practice

Cooperative Structure:
RallyTable

RallyTable is an excellent structure for guided practice. After introducing a decimal skill with manipulatives, pair students for additional practice using their textbook or an appropriate worksheet. Give each pair one worksheet and two different colored pencils for accountability. Have them take turns completing the worksheet using their own colored pencil. Remind students to watch their partners carefully and offer praise or help as needed.

ACTIVITY 12.4

Decimal Scavenger Hunt

Cooperative Structure:
RoundRobin

Several days before this activity, ask students to look for examples of decimals used in everyday life. Have them write down what they find, perhaps even bringing in newspaper clippings or product boxes. On the day of the activity, ask each person, in turn, to give a short report to their team explaining all the ways they discovered that decimals are used in the real world. You may want to set a time limit, such as 1 minute, for each person to speak.

Additional Activities

ACTIVITY
12.5

Checking Homework

Cooperative Structure:
RoundRobin

RoundRobin is an effective way to have students correct their homework. Ask one person on each team to start by reading their answer to the first problem. Team members give a thumbs-up if they agree or discuss the problem if they don't. Students are allowed to make corrections to their papers only after they understand their errors. As students work, circulate around the class to see if specific problems are causing everyone difficulty. Follow up by reviewing only those problems at the end of the RoundRobin homework session.

Additional Activities

Chapter 4

Patterns & Blacklines

Directions For Making Base 10 Place Value Mats

Directions:

1. Use a dark marker to divide an 18" x 24" piece of construction paper or poster board into sections as shown below.
2. Draw decimal points in three locations between the flats and the rods.
3. Cut out labels and glue in correct locations at the top of each column.
4. When using the manipulatives, the cubes represent the tens place, the flats are ones, the rods are tenths, and the units are hundredths.

Cubes	Flats	Rods	Units

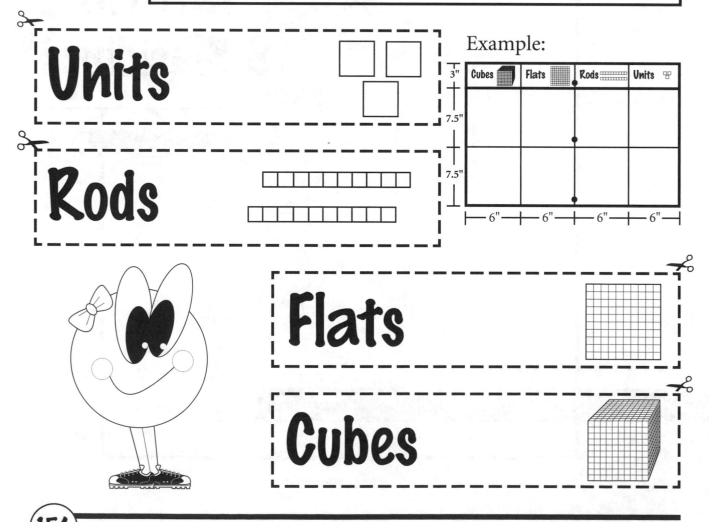

Units

Rods

Example:

Cubes	Flats	Rods	Units

3" 7.5" 7.5"

6" 6" 6" 6"

Flats

Cubes

Base 10 Manipulative Patterns for Overhead

Directions:
Make several copies on colored transparency film. Cut apart on dark lines only.

Units

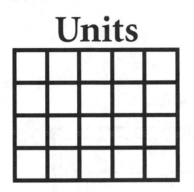

Rods

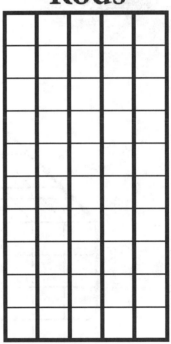

Flats

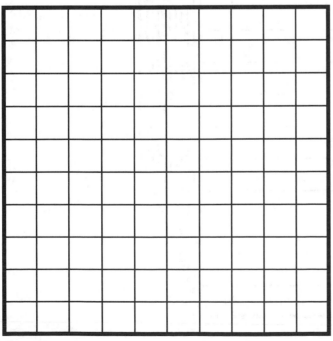

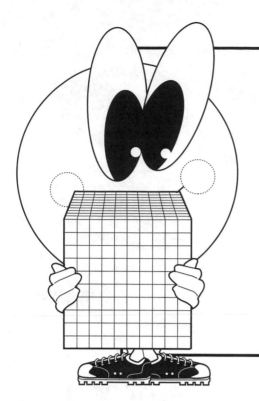

Base 10 Manipulative Cube Pattern

Directions:

Make as many copies as needed.
Cut apart on dark lines only.

Cubes

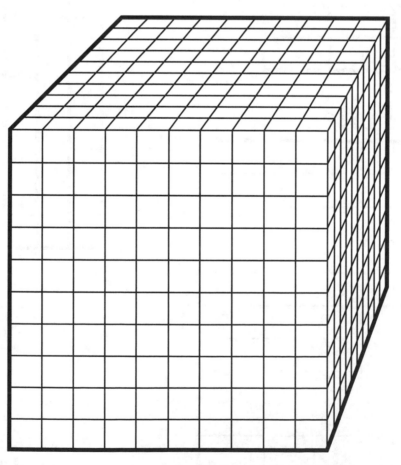

Decimal Squares
(Tenths)

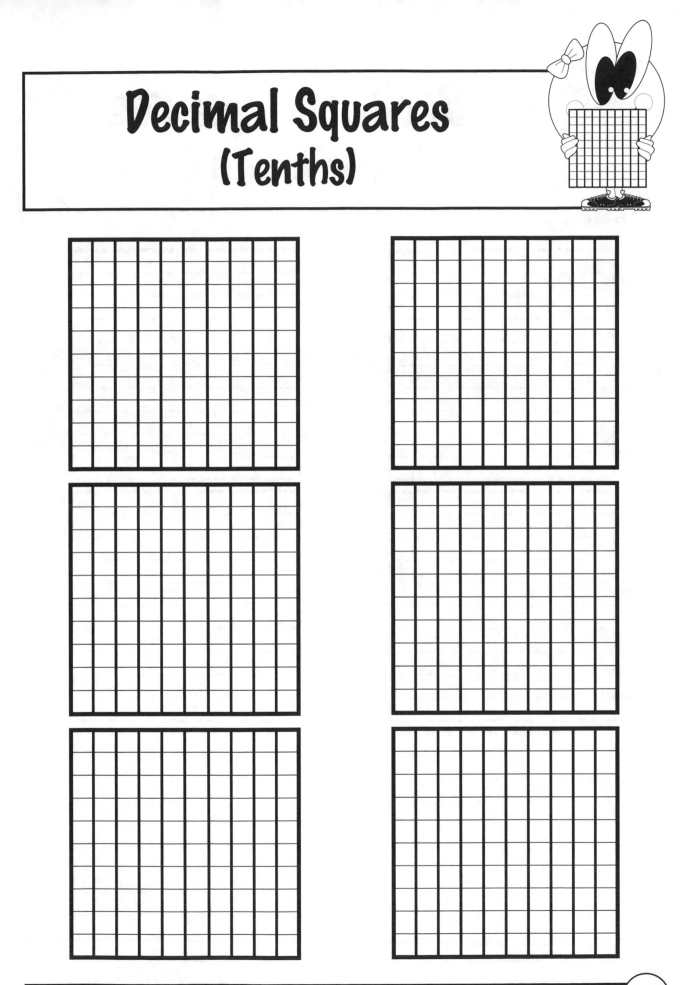

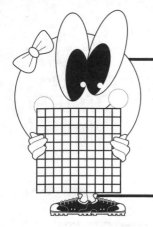

Decimal Squares
(Hundredths)

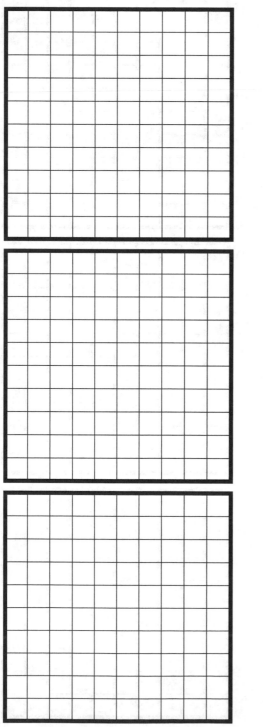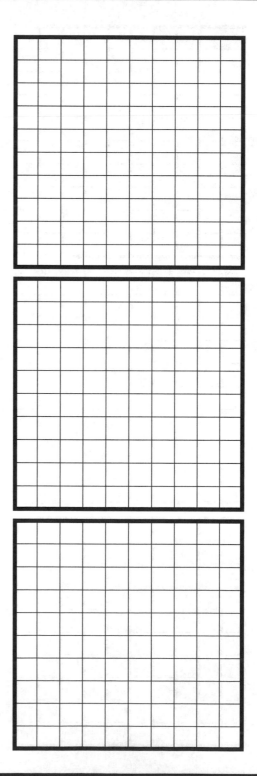

Discovering Decimals by Laura Candler • *Kagan Publishing* • 1 (800) 933-2667 • www.KaganOnline.com

Decimal Number Cards
Tenths

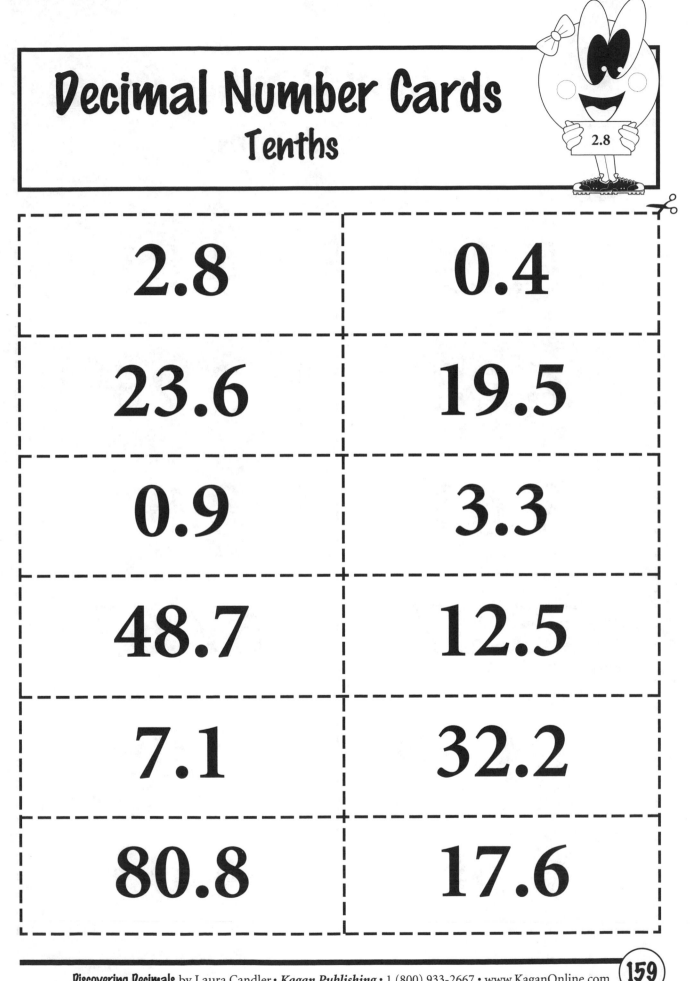

2.8	0.4
23.6	19.5
0.9	3.3
48.7	12.5
7.1	32.2
80.8	17.6

Decimal Number Cards
Hundredths

0.29	4.81
6.08	3.25
9.63	8.04
15.07	67.67
104.28	0.09
0.56	4.03

 Discovering Decimals by Laura Candler • *Kagan Publishing* • 1 (800) 933-2667 • www.KaganOnline.com

Decimal Number Cards
Thousandths

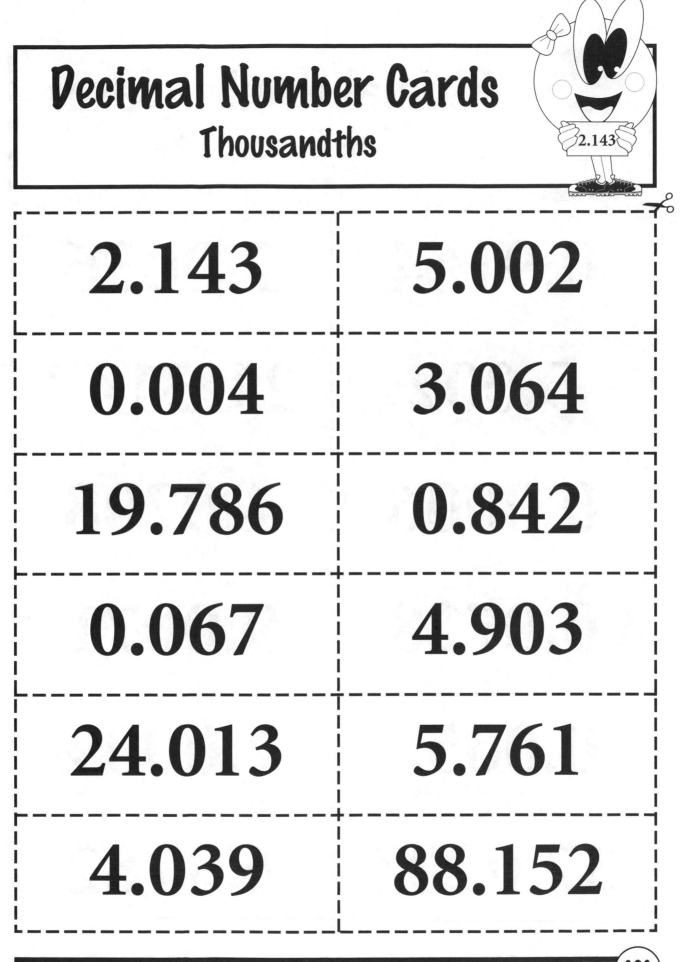

2.143

2.143	5.002
0.004	3.064
19.786	0.842
0.067	4.903
24.013	5.761
4.039	88.152

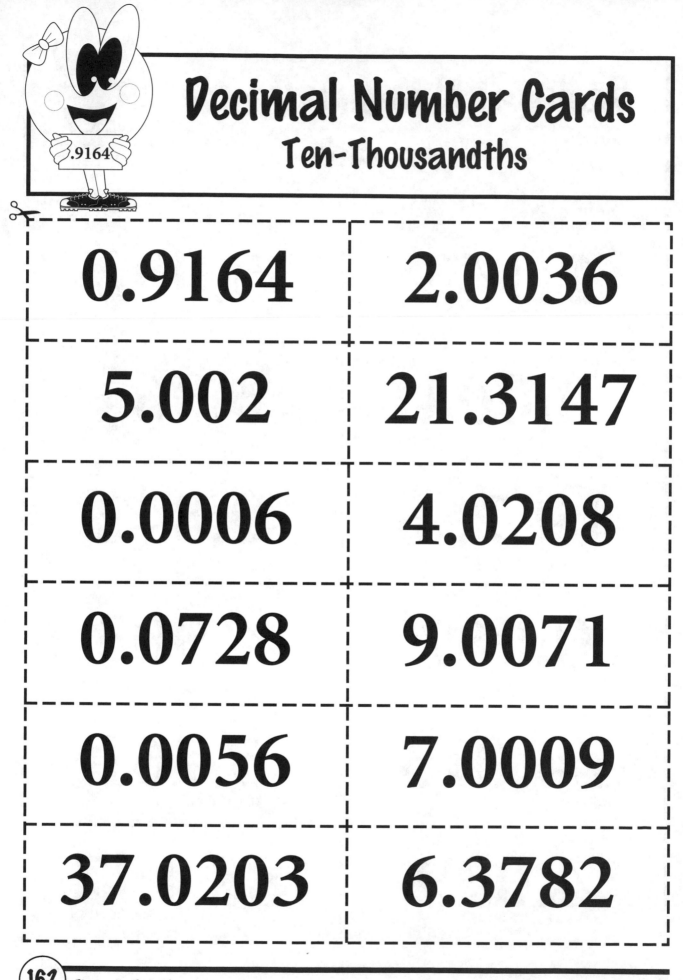

Decimal Number Cards
Ten-Thousandths

0.9164	2.0036
5.002	21.3147
0.0006	4.0208
0.0728	9.0071
0.0056	7.0009
37.0203	6.3782

.9164

 Discovering Decimals by Laura Candler • Kagan Publishing • 1 (800) 933-2667 • www.KaganOnline.com

Coins

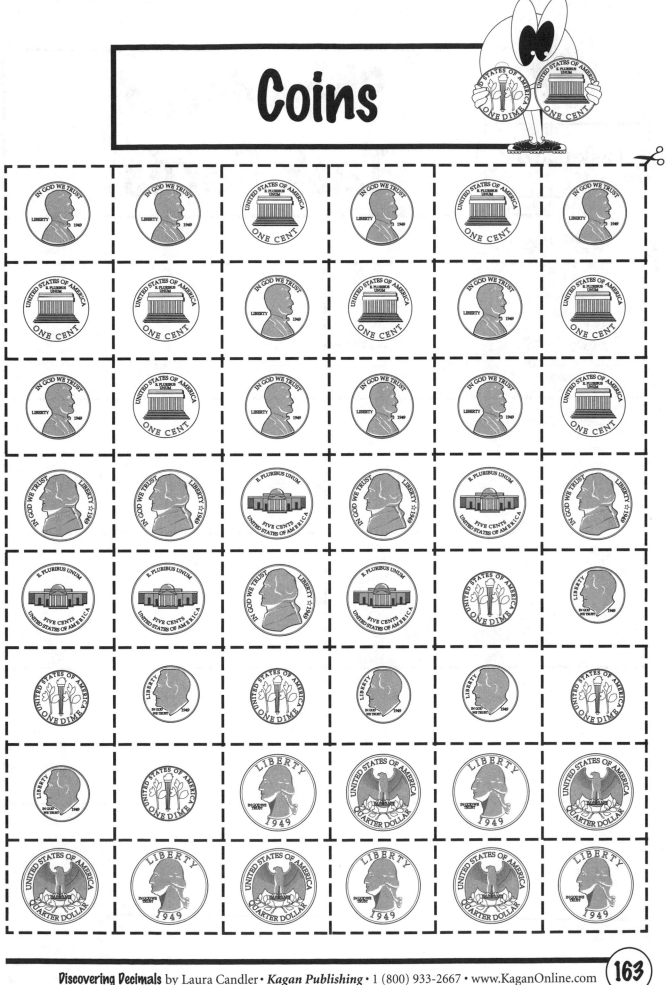

Showdown
Task Cards

Discovering Decimals by Laura Candler • *Kagan Publishing* • 1 (800) 933-2667 • www.KaganOnline.com

Pairs Check Form

Name _____   Name _____

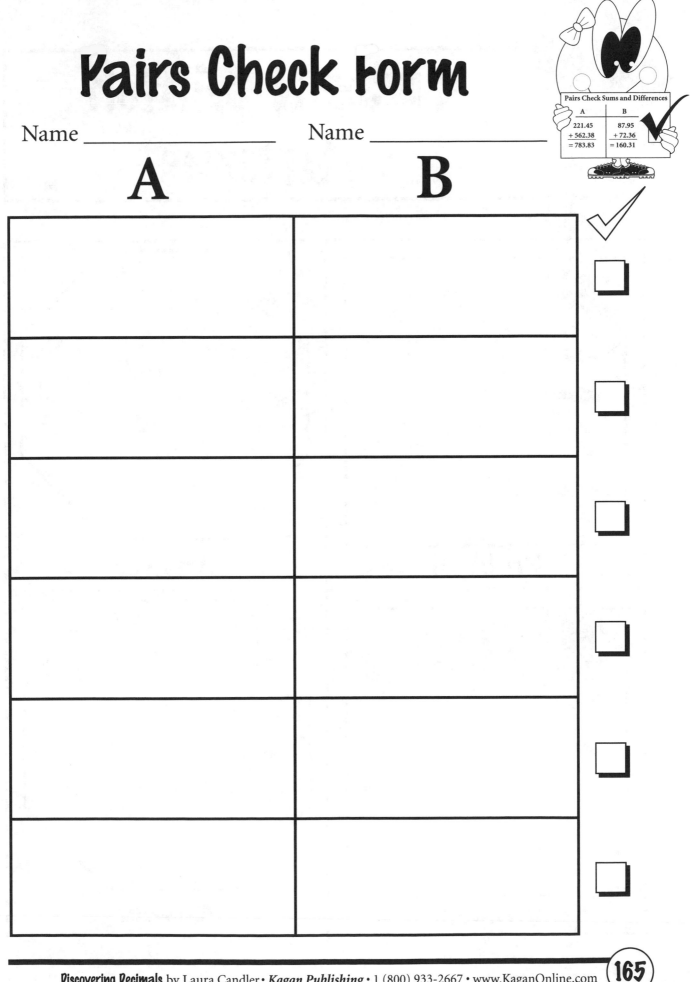

A	**B**	
		☐
		☐
		☐
		☐
		☐
		☐

Pairs Check Sums and Differences

A	B
221.45	87.95
+ 562.38	+ 72.36
= 783.83	= 160.31

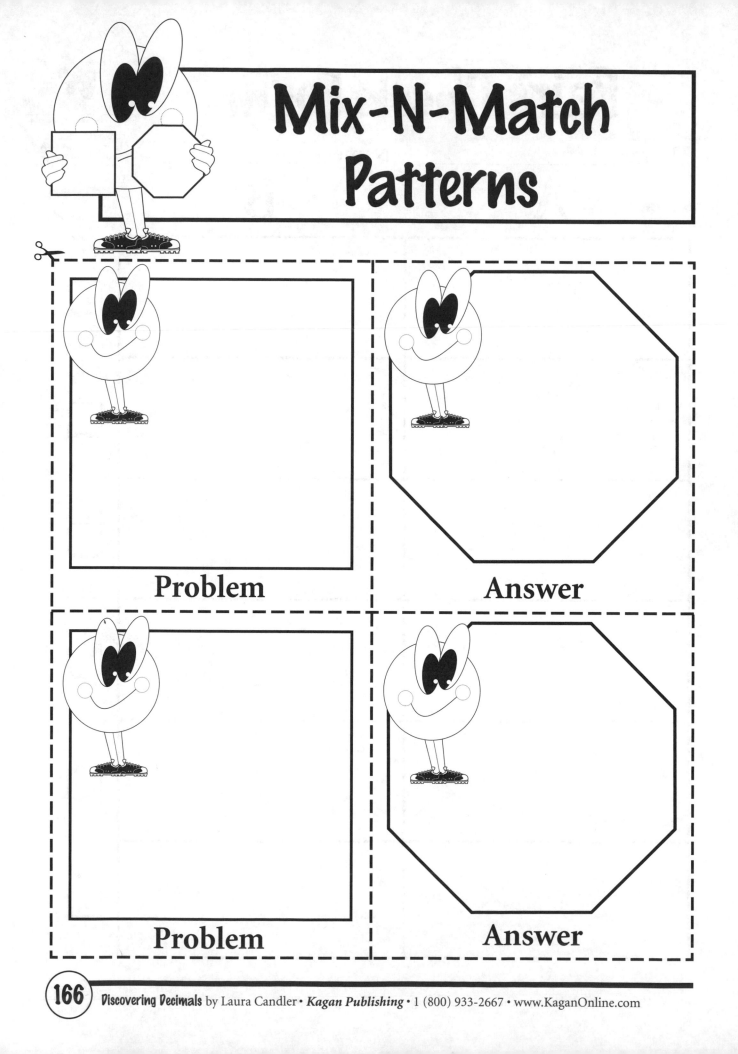

Mix-N-Match
Patterns

Problem

Answer

Problem

Answer

Chapter 5

Answers

Answers for Activities
2.4, 3.3, 4.3 & 7.2

ACTIVITY 2.4

RallyTable Decimal Writing

Name (A)_____ Name (B)_____

1)	Two and fifty-five hundredths	**2.55**
2)	Eighteen and seven tenths	**18.7**
3)	Two hundred fifteen and seventy-five hundredths	**215.75**
4)	Ninety-three hundredths	**0.93**
5)	Six and fourteen thousandths	**6.014**
6)	Three hundred twelve and twenty-two hundredths	**312.22**
7)	Seven and five hundred two thousandths	**7.502**
8)	Ninety and nineteen thousandths	**90.019**
9)	Eight tenths	**0.8**
10)	Forty-one and seven hundredths	**41.07**
11)	Seventy-two and eighty-three hundredths	**72.083**
12)	Four thousandths	**0.004**

What's The Order?

ACTIVITY 3.3

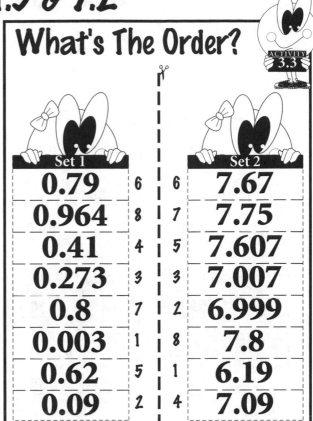

Set 1			Set 2
0.79	6	6	**7.67**
0.964	8	7	**7.75**
0.41	4	5	**7.607**
0.273	3	3	**7.007**
0.8	7	2	**6.999**
0.003	1	8	**7.8**
0.62	5	1	**6.19**
0.09	2	4	**7.09**

ACTIVITY 4.3

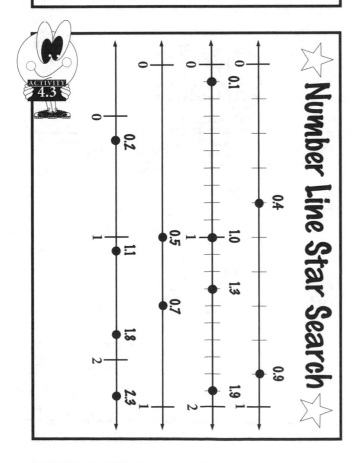

Number Line Star Search

Pairs Check Sums and Differences

ACTIVITY 7.2

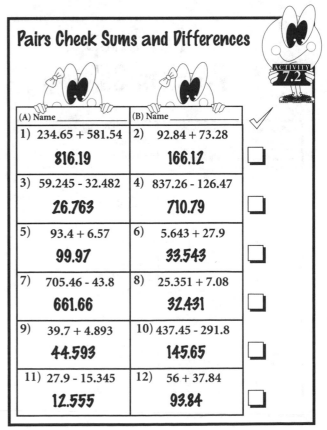

(A) Name _____	(B) Name _____	✓
1) 234.65 + 581.54 **816.19**	2) 92.84 + 73.28 **166.12**	☐
3) 59.245 - 32.482 **26.763**	4) 837.26 - 126.47 **710.79**	☐
5) 93.4 + 6.57 **99.97**	6) 5.643 + 27.9 **33.543**	☐
7) 705.46 - 43.8 **661.66**	8) 25.351 + 7.08 **32.431**	☐
9) 39.7 + 4.893 **44.593**	10) 437.45 - 291.8 **145.65**	☐
11) 27.9 - 15.345 **12.555**	12) 56 + 37.84 **93.84**	☐

Discovering Decimals by Laura Candler • *Kagan Publishing* • 1 (800) 933-2667 • www.KaganOnline.com

Answers for Activities
9.2, 10.1, 11.1 & 11.2

Purple Products

ACTIVITY 9.2

1) 0.3 x 0.3=

0.09

2) 0.3 x 0.9=

0.27

3) 0.8 x 0.6=

0.48

4) 0.1 x 0.7=

0.07

5) 0.5 x 0.6=

0.30

6) 0.4 x 0.9=

0.36

7) 0.8 x 0.2=

0.16

8) 0.7 x 0.5=

0.35

Decimals Into Fractions Task Cards

ACTIVITY 10.1

0.5 Team Answer $\frac{5}{10}=\frac{1}{2}$	0.25 Team Answer $\frac{25}{100}=\frac{1}{4}$
0.4 Team Answer $\frac{4}{10}=\frac{2}{5}$	0.20 Team Answer $\frac{20}{100}=\frac{1}{5}$
0.75 Team Answer $\frac{75}{100}=\frac{3}{4}$	0.8 Team Answer $\frac{8}{10}=\frac{4}{5}$
0.35 Team Answer $\frac{35}{100}=\frac{7}{20}$	0.05 Team Answer $\frac{5}{100}=\frac{1}{20}$
0.68 Team Answer $\frac{5}{10}=\frac{1}{2}$	0.16 Team Answer $\frac{16}{100}=\frac{4}{25}$

Pet Shop Problem Solving

ACTIVITY 11.1

1. Sonya and Donald work at Pet Paradise during the summer. One of Sonya's jobs is to keep the aquarium filled. The aquarium contains 18.7 gallons of water. If she adds 2.9 gallons, how many gallons will be in the aquarium in all?

Answer: **21.6 gallons**
Explanation: _____

2. Donald feeds the dogs each morning. This morning, the store owner gave him two bags of dog food—a full 5 pound bag and one weighing only 3.4 pounds. Donald was told to give each of the 14 dogs exactly the same amount of dog food. How much did he measure out for each dog?

Answer: **0.6 lb**
Explanation: _____

3. Pet Paradise sells bird seed for $1.20 a pound. Sonya poured three large scoops into a bag for a customer and found that it weighed 2.7 pounds. The same customer also bought a bird cage for $15.95. How much did the customer owe in all?

Answer: **$19.19**
Explanation: _____

4. Donald weighed each of Pet Paradise's four kittens. The first weighed 2.79 lbs, the second was exactly 3 lbs, the third was 2.65 lbs, and the last one weighed only 2.2 pounds. What was the average weight of a kitten at Pet Paradise?

Answer: **2.66 lbs**
Explanation: _____

Better Buy Bargains

ACTIVITY 11.2

Problems

1 Rebecca wants to buy cupcakes. She can buy 2 for $0.48 or 5 cupcakes for $1.25. Which is the better buy? Explain your answer.

2 for $0.48

2 Thomas is shopping for chicken. One brand has a 3 lb. package for $5.25. Another brand has a 2 lb. package for $3.60. Which package is the better buy? Explain your answer.

3lbs. for $5.25

3 A 2 liter bottle of Cola sells for $1.28 and a 3 liter bottle is $2.04. Which bottle is the better buy? Explain your answer.

2 L for $1.28

4 Judy found a 6 oz. can of orange juice for $0.72 and a 9 oz. can for $1.17. Which is the better buy and why?

6oz. for $0.72

5 Which is the better buy: a 5 oz. container of yogurt for $0.75 or an 8 oz. carton for $1.12? Explain your answer.

8 oz. for $1.12

6 Tonya wants to buy toothpaste. She can choose between a 6 oz. tube for $1.26 or an 8 oz. tube for $1.60. Which is the better buy and why?

8oz. for $1.60

7 Sweetsie Donuts are sold in 2 package sizes. One box contains 6 donuts for $0.72. The other box has a dozen for $1.92. Which is the better buy? Explain your answer.

6 for $0.72

8 Terry needs 8 oz. of tomato paste for her spaghetti sauce. Should she buy several 4 oz. cans costing $0.60 each or the 10 oz. can for $1.00? Explain your answer.

the 10oz. can for $1.00

Movie Madness

ACTIVITY 11.4

Word Problems

Problem 1
Jessica and her three friends went to see *Star Voyage* at Max's Movie House. How much did they pay in all for their tickets?

$17.00

Problem 2
Tamara's grandfather, a senior citizen, took her and her brother to the All Star Cinema. Tamara and her brother got children's tickets. How much did her grandfather pay in all?

$12.50

Problem 3
Mr. Thomas bought 2 children's tickets and 2 adult tickets at the Bargain Cinema. He paid with a $20 bill. How much change did he get back?

$3.50

Problem 4
Mrs. Avis took her 2 children to the movies and paid exactly $17.25 for the 3 tickets. Which movie theater did she take them to?

Bayview Cinema

Problem 5
Mrs. Davis invited four friends to the movies. Three of the ladies were senior citizens. Which theater would be the least expensive? How much would she pay in all?

Max's Movie House $21.25

Decimal Bingo Problem Cards Set 1

ACTIVITY 12.1

Add	Subtract
2.3 + 48.68	27.64 - 2.3
50.98	25.34
Divide	Round to the nearest hundredth 9.841
15.2 ÷ 4	
3.8	9.84
Solve	Which number is smaller?
5.098 x 100	7.1 or 7.35
509.8	7.1
Write the standard form Nine and eighty-five hundredths	Multiply 5.68 x 7
9.85	39.76
Round to the nearest tenth	Estimate 9.23
3.85	+4.9
3.9	14

Decimal Bingo Problem Cards Set 2

ACTIVITY 12.1

Estimate	Add
43.98 - 17.64	4.2 + 65.95 + 103.4
20	173.55
Round to the nearest whole number 13.261	Subtract
13	55 - 23.5
	9.84
Add 40.3 56.94 0.78 +25.6	Estimate
123.62	19.6 x 3
	60
Multiply 34.77 x 5	Divide
9.85	36.75 ÷ 5
	7.35
Estimate 79.7 ÷ 8	Which number is larger? 123.62 or 123.7
10	123.7

Notes...